145

THE BEAUTY OF
Big Cats

Triune Books

THE BEAUTY OF
Big Cats

by Howard Loxton

Acknowledgments

Photographs were supplied by the following

AFA: Page 11*l*, 11*cr*, 28*b*, 93, 116*b*, 124*br*, 125*t*, 143*t*; Ardea
Photographics: Page 17, 29*b*, 120*bl*; Barnaby's Picture Library:
Page 33*b*, 35*tr*, 35*tl*, 35*b*, 48*b*, 66*tr*, 73*br*, 75*c*, 84*t*, 88*b*, 92*l*, 94*t*,
95*t*, 98*bl*, 120*t*, 125*bl*, 143*br*, 143*bl*; Camera Press: Page 126*l*;
Bruce Coleman: Page 8, 9, 12*l*, 13*l*, 19*tr*, 21, 22*t*, 22*b*, 23*t*, 24,
28*t*, 31*tr*, 32, 34, 36*t*, 47*b*, 55*b*, 54–55*b*, 64*b*, 65*r*, 67, 68*b*, 69*t*, 71*tr*,
71*c*, 72, 74*tr*, 74*b*, 75*tr*, 75*br*, 76*tr*, 76*b*, 78*cl*, 78*bl*, 85, 88*t*, 91*bl*,
96*t*, 99*t*, 99*bl*, 99*br*, 102, 103*t*, 103*b*, 104*tl*, 104*tr*, 105, 107*t*, 107*bl*,
107*br*, 109*t*, 109*b*, 111*tl*, 111*br*, 113*t*, 113*b*, 114*t*, 114*b*, 115, 116*t*,
117*t*, 117*bl*, 117*br*, 118*b*, 120*c*, 121, 126*r*, 130*l*, 131*bl*, 131*br*, 133*t*,
134, 135*l*, 135*r*, 138*bl*, 138*br*, 139*br*, 141*t*, 141*b*, 144; Collins:
Page 98*t*; Jeffrey Craig: Page 60; Mary Evans Picture Library:
Page 122*tl*, 136*tl*, 136*bl*, 136*br*, 137*t*, 137*br*, 142; Griffith Institute:
Page 58, 59*l*; Michael Holford: Page 56, 63*br*; Geoffrey Kinns:
Page 15*tl*, 15*tr*, 104*b*; Frank Lane: Page 10, 11*br*, 25, 27*b*, 31*tl*, 31*br*,
49*b*, 54*t*, 54*b*, 66*l*, 68*t*, 70, 71*br*, 76*tl*, 77, 78*tl*, 78*r*, 90, 95, 110*tl*, 128*b*,
130*r*, 137*br*, 138*t*, 142*bl*; Howard Loxton: Page 60*r*, 80*l*, 124*l*;
Mansell Collection: Page 59*r*, 82, 87, 122*r*, 123, 136*tl*; National Film
Archive: Page 112; Natural Science Photos: Page 89; Axel
Poignant: Page 62, 110–111, 129; Radio Times Hulton Picture
Library: Page 41, 55*t*, 62*r*, 79, 83, 86*tl*, 91*tl*, 95*tr*, 110*tr*, 111*tr*, 122,
125*br*, 127*t*, 133*bl*; San Diego Zoo: Page 15*b*, 16*t*, 16*b*, 18*tl*, 19*tl*,
27*tr*, 28, 39*b*, 42*b*, 45, 58*b*, 63*t*, 96*bl*, 100*l*, 100*r*, 142*t*; Sotheby's:
Page 127*b*; Spectrum Colour Library: Page 7*l*, 7*r*, 18*tr*, 26*b*, 53,
57, 61*b*, 81, 92*r*, 98*br*, 101, 118*t*, 119*t*, 119*b*, 124*tr*, 133*br*, 140;
Sally Anne Thompson: Page 29*t*, 33*t*, 33*bl*, 36*b*, 73*t*, 73*c*, 73*bl*,
94*b*, 108, 131*t*; Victoria and Albert Museum: Page 91*r*; World
Wildlife Fund: Page 14*tl*, 20, 27*tl*, 30*t*, 39, 44*bl*, 44*br*, 47*t*, 50*t*, 50*b*,
52, 61*t*, 67*br*, 69*bl*, 75*l*, 139*bl*; Zoological Society of Bristol: Page
106*tl*, 106*tr*; Zoological Society of London: Page 1, 11*tr*, 12*r*, 13*r*,
14*tr*, 14*b*, 18*br*, 19*bl*, 19*br*, 23*b*, 26*t*, 30*bl*, 38*t*, 40, 46, 48*t*, 49*t*,
54*c*, 64*t*, 65*l*, 84*b*, 86*cl*, 86*b*, 103*t*, 110*bl*, 132, 139*t*

ISBN 0 85674 012 8
Published by
Triune Books, London, England
© Trewin Copplestone Publishing Ltd 1973
Printed in Great Britain by
Sir Joseph Causton & Sons Ltd
London & Eastleigh

Contents

Prehistoric cats

The cat family was one of the earliest groups of animals to develop into a form recognizably close to that we know today. It developed from an early type of carnivore (flesh-eater) which was also the common ancestor of the dog, the weasel, the racoon—and even of the bear.

Fossils show that 40 million years ago the animal which scientists call *Dinictis* looked very like our modern cats. It was about the size of a lynx, had cat-like teeth—with canines much larger than in modern cats, and retractile claws; but it had a smaller brain than modern cats.

There is no firm evidence, but it seems likely that from *Dinictis* two groups of animals developed. In one group the canine teeth grew smaller; they were the *Felinae* or typical cats, the group to which the cats of today belong. In the other group the canine teeth grew even bigger; they were the *Machairodontinae*, or sabre-toothed cats, which had heavy fore-quarters and relatively light hindquarters, making them slower moving than the *Felinae*. It is even possible that *Dinictis* itself should be included in this group, and that an earlier common ancestor of both groups existed.

Most startling and most advanced of the Machairodonts was the *Smilodon*, which ranged over the American continent from California to Pennsylvania, and south to Argentina and Brazil, during the Pleistocene, a million years ago. Best known of this North American species is *Smilodon californicus*, the remains of which have been found in great quantity in the Rancho La Brea asphalt pits of southern California.

In this area near Los Angeles, oil is forced up through the earth by the pressure of gases beneath, and on the surface it gradually oxidizes and evaporates until it becomes asphalt. At one stage in the process it acts like a huge, sticky flypaper, trapping any bird or animal that lights upon it. During the Pleistocene age, there were water pools above the soft tar which attracted animals to drink. Smaller animals which became trapped in the tar then became prey for older or injured predators, or inexperienced young carnivores, who in their turn became inextricably stuck in the tar and slowly perished, leaving their bones for us to study today. These bones show a high proportion of old, crippled or diseased animals. Their sabre-like teeth are also frequently damaged, and the worn condition of the broken ends shows that the injury was sustained long before death.

In *Smilodons*, these sabre-teeth extended beyond the lower jaw when it was closed, but in other sabre-tooth species, such as *Eusmilus* and *Hoplophoneus*, the protective flanges of the lower jaw made it impossible to use the tusks until the mouth was very wide open. In all cases, they were not used to bite with but to inflict a vicious, stabbing blow. In fact, the lower jaw was comparatively weak, but the neck muscles and those used to bring the head down could deliver a blow of enormous force.

Dinictis, *Eusmilus* and *Hoplophoneus* were all Old World species which reached North America from Asia. *Smilodon* and the other New World cats developed in North America and crossed to the southern half of the continent after the re-establishment of the Panamanian land bridge about one million years ago. The skeletons of an Argentinian species, *Smilodon neogaenus*, have been found in abundance in the loams of the Argentine pampas, and its predations are thought to have been largely responsible for the extinction of many of the earlier large South American mammals.

The last date for the Californian *Smilodon* is about 13,000 years ago, but in Europe the sabre-tooths disappeared much earlier. The last dated specimen was a species known as the Lesser Scimitar Cat (*Homotherium latidens*) of 30,000 years ago, found in Robin Hood's Cave in Derbyshire, England.

Contemporary with the *Smilodons*, and found with them in the Californian tar, are the bones of the so-called American lion, *Panthera atrox*, a huge cat that was a quarter larger than the present-day African lion. This species ranged from Alaska south to Florida and Texas, but no specimens have been discovered in South America. At Rancho La Brea they are out-numbered 30 to 1 among the remains, but this may not mean that they were any less common

The lion **left** and tiger **above** share a common ancestry with the sabre-tooth tiger and the domestic cat

than the sabre-tooths—rather, perhaps, that their more highly developed brains gave them the intelligence to avoid being fatally trapped.

This lion was almost certainly an immigrant from Asia—a supposition supported by the remains of *Panthera atrox* found in Alaska—and is closely related to the European Cave Lion, *Panthera leo spelaea*. The Cave Lion or its close relations were distributed across Europe into the western parts of Siberia, south through Africa and across south-east Asia as far as Ceylon. It was established in Britain 500,000 years ago and survived there until at least 450,000 years later. In Greece it is believed to have persisted until 480 BC, when lions attacked Xerxes' baggage train in Macedonia. The American species may have survived in California until about 4500 years ago.

The development of many of our extant species also dates back to the Pleistocene. The puma was established, the lynx had already reached America, the modern tiger spread through Asia (including Japan in its territory), and before the Ice Ages, the leopard ranged over the Old World territories of the lion and the tiger combined. Changing climate, movement of prey and the action of human beings have all affected the distribution and survival of these species into modern times.

This lioness's prehistoric ancestors ranged across Europe, Africa, Asia and through Alaska into North America. **Opposite page** Cheetah with cubs, their woolly coat and silvery mane disappear as their spots become more prominent

The cat family

The present-day members of the cat family *Felidae* all belong to the subfamily of typical cats, the *Felinae*. They are distinguished, as the *Encyclopedia Britannica* puts it, 'by the position of the posterior palatine foramina on the maxillopalatal suture and the absence of the interramal tuft of vibrissæ.' More obvious to the layman is the fact that they all look like cats and, from the largest lion to the smallest domestic pet curled up before the fire, are recognizably members of the same family, with many characteristics in common.

They are, of course, flesh-eaters and in nature hunt for living prey. They have strong and agile bodies with short muzzles and supple forelegs. They are light-footed and walk on their toes. They have acute hearing and highly developed vision which enables them to see in poor light. Their tongues are covered with a rasp-like surface which they use to scrape flesh from bones and in grooming their coats. Their teeth are designed for grasping prey and cutting meat, but not for grinding. They have special bristle-like hairs, called vibrissæ, in the form of face whiskers and on the rear of the forelegs, which have a sensory function that is not yet understood. And their claws can be retracted into protective sheaths.

It used to be considered that all cats except the cheetah belonged to the same genus, but today four separate genera are recognized. The two largest groups are *Felis* and *Panthera*. They are differentiated by the development of one of the bones (called hyoid) at the base of the tongue, which in the *Panthera* forms only a thread-like ligament so that the tongue and larynx are quite loosely attached to the base of the skull. This means that the vocal apparatus can move freely, enabling the large *Panthera* to roar, whilst the *Felis* group, which contains the medium and small-size cats, can only make comparatively feeble cries.

The other genera consist of only one species each:
Neofelis, the Clouded Leopard (or Clouded Tiger), has very long upper canine teeth which set it apart. In both physiology and behavior it falls somewhere between the two main genera. *Acinonyx*, the Cheetah, has a hyoid like the *Felis* group but its claws are only partly retractile. The *Lynx* is also sometimes classified as a separate genus. Its short tail, tufted ears and a difference in tooth arrangement set it apart.

This book is mainly concerned with the Big Cats which belong to the *Panthera*, but as all members of the cat family have so much in common, each variety, large or small, will be described and compared in the following section.

9

Cheetah

Acinonyx jubatus

A fully-grown cheetah is just over four feet long, plus an extra two feet of tail, and stands about thirty inches high at the shoulder. Its small head is rounded and a little dog-like, with short ears, and its legs are very long compared with other cats. The cheetah has the vocal apparatus of the smaller cats of the genus *Felis*, but lies down with its paws stretched out in front like the big cats of the genus *Panthera* (the smaller cats tuck their paws in). It differs from every other member of the cat family in that its claws are not fully retractile once cubs are about ten weeks old.

Cubs have a smoky gray coat of long woolly hair with a silver mane running down the length of their back which disappears after their tenth week, as the coat becomes yellowish on the legs and sides, and spots develop until it attains the rough adult coat which ranges from tawny on the back to almost white on the belly. Most of the body is covered with solid black spots, set close together and merging into black bands towards the end of the tail, which has a bushy white tip. There is a further black stripe from the corner of the eye to the edge of the mouth, where it widens into a blob. The tip of the ear is splashed with white and the fur on neck and shoulders is thicker than elsewhere, forming an incipient mane. A variant form has been found in Rhodesia which has broad, irregular stripes along the back and diagonally across the flanks. It has been given the name King Cheetah, and is sometimes classified as a separate species, *Acinonyx rex*.

The Cheetah used to range from Morocco, across North Africa, Iran and Afghanistan to India, and south through Africa wherever there was suitable, open, semi-arid country. But it has not been recorded in India since 1948, and the extension of agriculture has limited its natural prey, making it rare elsewhere, though still relatively abundant in parts of East Africa.

The cheetah is the fastest four-legged animal on earth and over short distances can reach speeds of 60 mph. One record even shows a speed of 71 mph over 700 yards, and it has been claimed that they can accelerate to 45 mph in only two seconds. However, they cannot sustain such speeds over long distances. Their body conformation is designed to facilitate these bursts of speed and in addition to their deep chest and long legs, their claws are blunt and only slightly curved and their forelimbs are unable to rotate as freely as in other cats.

Cheetah making a meal of a Grant's gazelle

Although the backward and forward motion helps them to run faster, it also limits their mobility when prey takes evasive action.

The cheetah hunts by day, usually in the morning or evening, when it is cooler, or by moonlight, and its prey consists of gazelles, impala and other small antelopes (black buck and axis deer in Asia), hares, ostriches, guinea-fowl and other game-birds. Larger animals such as zebra and wildebeest may be taken when cheetah hunt in groups.

Usually cheetahs are solitary but they sometimes hunt in pairs, or in small family groups made up of males or males and females, but no groups consisting of females only have been observed.

For hundreds of years, cheetahs have been trained as hunting animals in India and North Africa, and with their timid disposition they have also been kept as pets, but it was not until 1960 that they were successfully bred in captivity.

Cubs are usually born in litters of two to four after a gestation period of just over thirteen weeks. Observations in East Africa suggest that in the wild the mortality rate is high–probably half do not survive their first year. Cubs make a birdlike chirrup which develops into a mew like that of domestic cats grown bigger; they purr, and growl when alarmed or annoyed.

Lynx
Felis lynx

The lynx is a medium-sized cat about three to three-and-a-half feet long in the body with a short tail about five to eight inches long. It has a flat head, and longish limbs compared with its short body, the hind-legs being longer than the forelegs. A full-grown animal will weigh up to forty pounds.

The coat ranges from a sandy gray to a tawny red with white underparts. In the summer the fur is thin and spotted with black but in the winter it becomes soft and dense and the spots usually disappear. There are long black tufts on the ears and cheek ruffs which move outwards when the cat hisses, compensating for the shortness of the tail, which other cats use to signal their anger.

At one time the lynx ranged through all the northern forests of the world but today the Eurasian lynx is rare in Europe outside Scandinavia and northern Russia, though it ranges across Asia as far as the Pacific coast of Siberia and as far south as the Himalaya. However, at least eight different races of this genus have been recorded and some survive in Greece, in the Carpathian mountains and possibly in the Massif Central of France.

The Spanish Lynx *(Lynx pardina)* is a smaller species with a more rounded tail than the other subspecies, and shorter fur which is covered all over with diamond-shaped spots. Once ranging over most of Spain and Portugal, it is now localized in the Coto Donana reserve in southern Spain.

Top left European lynx. **Top right** Northern lynx with two-month old cubs. **Middle** Siberian lynx. **Above** Canadian lynx

The Canadian Lynx *(Lynx canadensis)* is larger, with longer fur that is sometimes almost white and lacks spots. It can still be found through the northern forests of America.

Lynxes are solitary animals and hunt alone at night in the forests which they seldom leave. They prey on hares, rabbits, mice, rats, chipmunks, lemmings, squirrels, foxes, birds, fish (lynx are excellent swimmers) and even beetles. In North America, the snowshoe rabbit forms the major part of their diet. Their very broad feet enable the lynx to move easily over soft ground and snow so that in the winter they have an advantage over some bigger animals and may even attack a moose or reindeer.

Mating takes place in the spring and a litter of two to four kittens is born after a gestation period of about nine weeks (slightly less for the Canadian lynx). By the time winter comes, the kittens still have immature claws and have not cut their second set of teeth, so that they remain dependent on their mother for survival.

The lynx's call is somewhat like the night howl of a domestic tomcat—only louder.

The Caracal and the Bobcat are closely related species.

Caracal
Felis caracal

This most powerful of the smaller cats of Africa is also known as the African lynx or Desert lynx and is very like its northern relation in appearance. About two-and-a-half feet long with a ten-inch tail, it stands up to eighteen inches at the shoulder and may weigh up to forty pounds. It has a flat head and long limbs with the hindlegs longer than the forelegs. It has the ear tufts but not the cheek ruffs of the lynx.

The coat is short-haired and thick, an even grizzled reddish fawn to blackish, without markings on the body but with faint spots on the legs and lighter underparts. The ears are blackish and the ear tufts black, while the face has white markings and a black stripe between the eye and nose and a black spot on the side of the muzzle. Kittens are at first bright reddish brown but then grow silvery hairs, making them grayer than the adult cat.

The caracal ranges through the savannah lands and semi-desert of Africa, into Arabia and Afghanistan and India, but is becoming scarce in much of its range, particularly in Asia. It likes open, mountainous or sparsely-bushed

The caracal, also known as the African lynx or Desert lynx, has the ear tufts of the lynx but lacks its ruff

country but keeps away from forests. In hilly country it will often take refuge among boulders during the day, for it usually hunts at night, though occasionally by day if it is cloudy and cool.

It preys on small antelopes, monkeys, hares, rodents, lizards and birds, which it will often catch in flight for it can leap high into the air. Caracals have even been known to kill large eagles and are reputed to kill snakes. They will also take sheep and goats where they are available. They are excellent climbers.

Kittens are born in litters of two to four, sometimes five, after a gestation period of nine weeks and are hidden in a disused burrow or ant-bear hole, a rock crevice or a hollow tree.

Serval

Felis serval

This slender, long-legged cat grows to about three feet body length with a shortish, one-foot tail. It stands about twenty inches high at the shoulder and its small head is set on a long neck. Its large ears are oval and upstanding.

The tawny coat is handsomely marked with black spots which merge into elongated stripes on the neck and shoulders and rings on the tail. The longer fur on the underside is light buff or almost white.

The serval ranges through Africa wherever there are open savannahs. It likes lightly-bushed country, particularly marshy places and gullies with long grass or reeds. It will live in forest fringes and on high mountain moorlands but avoids arid land and must be within easy reach of water. In West Africa there is a color variation known as the Servaline or small-spotted serval which was once thought to be a separate species. This variation has a grayer coat speckled with small spots and is found chiefly in the savannahs of Guinea and on the edges of forests, and may occur in the same litter as the large-spotted variety.

The serval hunts a wide variety of prey: cane rats, lizards, francolins, guineafowl, even smaller antelope like steenbucks, and hares which their light build enables them to chase, cheetah-fashion. They are also said to eat vegetables and fish and have been observed digging mole rats from their burrows. They hunt largely at night and spend most of the day lying up in a disused burrow or among thick bushes or reeds. They are good climbers and will take refuge in a tree if pursued by enemies such as dogs.

They litter in a disused ant-bear or porcupine burrow, a rock crevice or a hollow in a clump of grass, and give birth to two to four kittens after a gestation period of about two-and-a-half months. They have a shrill call that sounds like a plaintive 'Mwa, mwa' repeated several times in succession.

The serval's large ears are set close together on the top of its head

Golden cat
Felis aurata

This extremely elusive cat is robustly built with about thirty inches body length, plus more than half as much again in tail. Its legs are comparatively short and it stands about twenty inches high at the shoulder.

The short, soft coat shows considerable variation in color, but is usually a deep golden brown, tending to a reddish tinge; but some animals are gray-blue, or even a blackish gray. The longer fur of the underparts is lighter, sometimes almost white, and usually has conspicuous dark spots which are even darker on the body. The rounded ears are black inside and the face is striped.

The golden cat lives on the fringes of high forests of West Africa, on the edge of the Guinea savannah and sometimes high in the mountains. It makes a den below ground and feeds on birds, rodents and rock hyraxes.

Temminck's golden cat
Felis temmincki

This Asian cat is closely related to the golden cat of Africa and is similar in character. Its body coat is usually an unrelieved color of rich golden-brown in contrast to the head which is patterned with white, black and gray stripes. The belly is paler and has black markings.

Temminck's Golden Cat ranges from the foothills of the Himalaya across to western China and south to Sumatra. It preys on rodents, fowl and small deer. It is extremely retiring and little is known about it.

European wild cat
Felis silvestris

The wild cat is very similar in appearance to the domestic tabby but is considerably stronger and larger, growing to as much as three feet in length. It is closely related to the domestic cat and can interbreed with it, but can be distinguished by its broad, untapered tail with a rounded tip. Its head is large and square and well-whiskered. The yellowish-gray coat has a dark streak running the length of the back and the bushy tail, and there are dark stripes on the sides. The underparts are whitish. Once common throughout all the wooded parts of Europe except Ireland, it is now known only in remote areas well away from man.

Wild cats are expert climbers but hunt on the ground, usually at night, preying on birds and rodents. On the west coast of Scotland they have been observed clawing fish out of the water at low tide and appear to have adopted a fish diet there. They make a den in caves and crevices, under tree roots, or in a hollow trunk.

Temminck's golden cat has distinctive facial markings

Kittens are born in the spring in litters of three to six after 68 days' gestation. They are sexually mature at less than a year.

Scottish wild cat. The rounded tip of the tail is typical. Like all the genus *felis*, the wildcat's

tongue is covered with coarse papillæ and the pupils of the eyes narrow to a slit

African wild cat
Felis libyca

The African wild cat is slightly larger than the average domestic cat, being fourteen inches at the shoulder and weighing up to fourteen pounds.

The coat is gray to tawny yellow, reddish behind the ears and with pale underparts. The legs and long tail are broadly striped and the body marked with stripes and blotches in tabby pattern. There is a wide variation in color. Animals living in forests and wet areas are usually darker than those in more arid territories. The African wild cat, also known as the Kaffir cat and the Egyptian cat, ranges through all types of savannah in Africa and in parts of south-west Asia. Its remains have been found in caves at Gibraltar and it may once have shared part of the territory of the European wild cat, to which it is closely related. *Felis libyca* was probably one of the direct ancestors of the domestic cat. It can itself be domesticated and can breed with domestic cats and with *Felis sylvestris*. The mummified remains of this cat have been found in Egyptian tombs and temples.

A nocturnal hunter, preying on hares, rodents, snakes, lizards, birds and small antelope, it remains hidden during the day. It will also eat fruit and insects.

Litters of two to five kittens are born after a gestation period of 56 days. The call is a harsher version of the domestic cat's mew.

Jungle cat
Felis chaus

A larger cat than the African wild cat with long legs, a short tail and pointed ears, its general color is a grizzled fawn, reddish along the spine with the underparts and face a paler buff and the tail more gray. The ears are reddish brown and have long black hairs at their tips, but are not so tufted as the lynx and caracal. The body is indistinctly spotted, the legs have dark bands and the tail has two black bands close to its black tip.

This species ranges across Asia from the Caucasus to India and Vietnam. It also lives in north-east Africa in the Nile delta and the lower part of the Nile valley. It likes low, marshy ground, with reeds, sugar cane or bamboo to give cover, and it is also known as the Swamp Cat. It is a nocturnal hunter and will attack all kinds of small game.

Jungle cat

15

Black-footed cat

Black-footed cat
Felis nigripes

The Black-footed cat is smaller than many domestic cats, being about ten inches in shoulder height when fully grown. It has short legs, a short, bushy tail and oval ears which are slightly pointed at the tip. Its coat is a pale tawny color shading to nearly white on the belly and inside of the limbs. The body is covered with dark rounded spots which become transverse stripes on the shoulder. The tail has a black tip and the legs are encircled by three dark bands and have black underparts.

Distribution is limited to one area of southern Africa encompassing Botswana, the Kalahari desert and the western part of the Orange Free State. This cat is rare and little is known about it.

Sand cat
Felis margarita

This is another small cat, about ten inches at the shoulder. It is particularly distinguished by its broad face, made to look even wider by its large, low-set ears. Sandy in color, darkest on the spine and shading to almost white on the belly, it has a white face and is indistinctly marked with stripes and blotches that show more clearly in young animals. The tail is ringed and there are dark stripes on the upper legs.

It is also known as the Sahara cat and its range is limited to small areas of that desert, where it burrows in dunes under scrub and feeds on rodents, hares and birds.

Chinese desert cat
Felis bieti

This native of south-east Asia, from southern Mongolia through Kansu to Szechwan, lives in desert and semi-desert. It is very like the African wild cat *(Felis libyca)* but of slightly greater length and with a slight ear tuft.

Marbled cat
Felis marmorata

This cat is like a smaller replica of the clouded leopard. It is a little larger than a domestic cat and more heavily furred. Its large irregular markings are darkest on its spine and rear. It is thought to be a tree-dweller, and ranges from Nepal through south-east Asia to the islands of Borneo and Sumatra. Like the similar Bay cat *(Felis badia)* it feeds on rats, chickens, squirrels, birds and frogs, and is very fierce.

Above Marbled cats. **Opposite page** Canadian lynx

Flat-headed cat

Bay cat
Felis badia

This very rare cat lives only in dense forest in Borneo and has a marbled coat like the marbled cat *(Felis marmorata)*. It is small and long-tailed, the tail having a white streak on the underside and a black tip.

Flat-headed cat
Felis planiceps

This cat is up to two feet long, plus a short tail of about six inches, weighing from four to five-and-a-half pounds. Its broad head appears flattened.

Its fur is thick and a uniform grizzled dark brown on the body with a buff-colored head marked with white over the eyes.

The flat-headed cat lives by streams and on river banks in southern Asia, Borneo and Sumatra. It is nocturnal and lives on fish and fruit but does not often eat meat, apart from frogs.

Leopard cat
Felis bengalensis

A beautiful smaller cat, about the size of a domestic cat, with large appealing eyes and round, upstanding ears. Its coat is a grayish fawn spotted with black, the spots becoming elongated into stripes along the back and on the head. The underside is slightly paler and there are white flashes behind the ears.

The leopard cat can be found in south-east Asia and in the Philippines, and lives in forest and grassland and on river banks. A nocturnal hunter, it preys on birds and small mammals. It is thought to be entirely ground-dwelling.

Fishing cat
Felis viverrina

Another small cat, from one-and-a-half to two-and-a-half feet long, plus one foot of tail and similar to the leopard cat. Its grey-brown coat is marked with black spots which tend to form longitudinal lines. It lives in forests and grassland from India and Ceylon through south-east Asia to Java and Sumatra. It does catch and eat fish but it also feeds on large snails and other small prey.

Above A young leopard cat retaining the fluffy fur of kittenhood. **Top** Adult leopard cat

Fishing cat. Snails and other small prey also form part of its diet

Rusty-spotted cat

Felis rubiginosa

Similar to the leopard and fishing cats, this species ranges through southern India and Ceylon.

Pallas' cat

Felis manul

The manul cat, or Pallas' cat as it is called after the man who first described it, is about twenty inches long, the size of a domestic cat. It has a short, nine-inch tail, with a thick bushy end and a wide flat-topped head, accentuated by low-set ears and eyes that are both higher and more forward placed than in other cats. It has a long, soft coat which may be either a silvery gray or light buff, usually darker on the chest, and has light underparts. There are black rings on the tail and rear quarters and the cheeks are streaked with black. Some of the long body hairs are white with black tips and this increases the silvery

appearance. The fur is especially long near the tail and twice as long on the underparts— providing good insulation from the frozen ground when lying down.

Pallas' cat is comparatively rare but can be found in Tibet, Mongolia and parts of Siberia. It preys on small mammals and birds and it has been suggested that its low-set ears and high-set eyes are an adaptation developed to make it safer and easier to peer over rock ledges when it is hunting.

Left and above Pallas' cat. The placing of the ears and the distinctive face immediately identify this species

Above Caracal, or African lynx. Its short-haired coat may range from reddish fawn to blackish fawn. **Opposite page** Bobcat, North American relation of the lynx

Cougar

Felis concolor

This cat, which is also commonly known as the puma, the panther or the mountain lion, can be as large as five feet long in the body with a three-foot tail (in the biggest recorded specimen, which weighed 260 pounds), or as short as four feet, including tail, and forty-six pounds weight. There are at least fifteen different races—in fact thirty subspecies have been named—the larger ones living in the cooler climates and the smaller ones in the tropics. There is also a wide variation in the color of its short, close fur, which varies from yellow to yellowish brown or red.

The cougar's territory ranges right through the Americas from British Columbia in the north

to Tierra del Fuego in the south, in forests, plains, deserts and mountains.

This is a strong and powerful cat: the larger races can jump twelve feet into the air and cover twenty feet in a single leap – forty feet has been recorded on one occasion! An expert hunter, it will feed on anything from small rodents to adult deer and when they are available deer make up more than half its diet. It is a solitary animal and females will care for their young until they are two years old and siblings may hunt together for a short time.

Cougars breed at any time of year and produce a litter of one or two, or occasionally four, cubs after a gestation period of about thirteen weeks. The young are born with a black-ringed tail and are heavily spotted but the markings fade as they mature.

Bobcat
Felis rufus

This American cat is smaller than its close relation the lynx and usually carries less than half its weight, averaging about seventeen pounds, although exceptional specimens have been known which have weighed nearly forty pounds. An average body length is about two-and-a-half feet, plus six inches of tail. Its legs are shorter than those of the lynx and its feet, which do not have to cope with the snows of the northern winter, are not so large. It has the ear tufts and cheek ruff of the lynx and a short tail,

21

though in proportion the tail is somewhat longer and the ear tufts reduced in size.

Its coat is spotted like the European lynx and has a ground color from buff to tawny brown mixed with gray and white. The tail has a black bar on the upper side which is fringed with white hairs. The backs of the ears are white.

The bobcat's range includes southern Canada, through the United States into Mexico. It replaces the Canadian lynx, which lives in the coniferous forests to the north, but it is not found in the corn-belt across the midwest of the USA. It makes its home in rocky screes, thickets or swamps and does not usually range far from its den, unless food is scarce, when it may range over an area fifty miles across.

Bobcats hunt alone, and usually at night. They prey on a wide variety of animals including rodents, such as squirrels, deermice and voles, birds and rabbits. Snakes, skunks, grasshoppers and fruit are sometimes eaten and the bobcat's considerable strength in relation to its size also enables it to take deer (the white-tail is a large part of its diet in some areas) and domestic

The Bobcat usually hunts at night

22

livestock. This has caused the bobcat to be hunted and trapped but it has also been persecuted for its fur and chased, like a fox, for sport. Its size and adaptability have been responsible for its survival under these conditions.

Litters may consist of up to four kittens, although two is the usual number. They are born after a gestation period of about eight weeks. Male bobcats help to raise their kittens, aiding the female in collecting food, but are not allowed near them until they have been weaned.

Ocelot
Felis pardalis

The long-legged ocelot grows to as much as four feet in body length, plus fifteen inches of tail, and to a weight of thirty-five pounds, standing about eighteen inches at the shoulder. Its short-haired coat shows considerable color variation, ranging from light gray or yellowish gray to a rich brown, marked with rows of irregular sized brown blotches, rimmed with black, which become black streaks on the head and chest. Their ears are marked with white at the rear.

The ocelot can be found from the south-west of the United States, through Central America and south to Paraguay. Its name is a simplification of the native Mexican word *tlalocelotl*. It can swim well and is an expert climber, catching birds and small mammals found in trees, but does most of its hunting on the forest floor, and sometimes hunts in pairs. In areas where it has been left undisturbed by man, it is a

Ocelot

daylight animal but has become nocturnal where it has been hunted for its fine fur. Prey consists of agoutis, monkeys, rodents, brocket deer, birds and reptiles. In one recorded case it took on a seven-foot boa constrictor.

Kittens are born in litters of two and there are believed to be two breeding seasons a year. The call is like that of a noisy domestic cat.

Their handsome appearance has made the ocelot much sought after as a house pet and they can be domesticated, but may become unpredictable and dangerous when fully grown.

Margay
Felis wiedi

The margay is very like the ocelot and closely related to it, but smaller in size and build – about two feet long with an eighteen-inch tail and about thirteen pounds in weight. It has a rounder head than the ocelot and very big eyes.

Its soft fur is a bright tawny yellow, spotted and blotched in black. Margays range from the south-west of Texas through South America east of the Andes as far as Paraguay. They are extremely handsome, and young animals have often been reared as pets.

Jaguarondi
Felis jaguarondi

The jaguarondi is the most weasel-like of cats, with a long body and short legs and wide, flattened head with small low-set ears.

The coat is almost plain but may have indistinct blotches and stripes. It can be either rufous or gray, both types belong to the same species.

Leopard cat

Jaguarondi range from the southern frontiers of the United States through Central America to Paraguay, living on forest fringes and in savannah grasslands. Despite their short legs they climb easily and run fast over quite long distances. Their main prey are birds, especially ground-dwelling ones like the tinamous of Mexico. They will also eat fruit such as green figs, which they take directly from the tree.

Pampas cat
Felis pajeros
Another South American cat, about two-and-a-half feet long, plus ten inches of tail, it lives in the open pampas lands. The coat is yellowish gray with brown or straw-colored markings. The long, coarse fur grows long down the spine,

Margay

creating a distinct crest which is usually of a darker color.

Geoffroy's cat
Felis geoffroyi
Another small South American cat, which has a pale yellowish-gray coat with white underparts, which is spotted or streaked all over the body with black and has a black ringed tail.

Mountain cat
Felis jacobita

Tiger cat
Felis tigrina

Kodkod
Felis guigna
Three more small South American cats. The tiger cat is spotted and like a miniature version

of the margay. The kodkod is similar to the pampas cat, but a little smaller, and makes its home in wooded highlands such as the Chilean cordillera.

The margay's markings closely resemble those of the larger ocelot

Lion

Panthera leo

A fully-grown lion may be as long as eight feet in the body, plus another three feet of tail, stand more than three feet at the shoulder and weigh up to 450 pounds. An average beast would probably be about nine feet from nose to tail tip. The lion is built for strength rather than speed. His long body rests on short legs and he is powerfully muscled, particularly in the shoulders and forelegs. Females are smaller and more lightly built.

The coat is short and uniform in color, which may range from a pale sand to a dark ochreous brown. The underparts are lighter (in females almost white) and the head darker than the rest of the body. The backs of the ears are marked with black and there is a black tuft at the end of the long tail. Some, but by no means all, male lions have a mane. This may be no more than a fringe of longer hair around the face, but at its most luxuriant it covers all the head (except the face), neck and shoulders, continuing as a deep ruff across the chest to link with a fringe of long hair on the underside of the belly. The mane is not fully grown until the lion is about five years old. It may range from silvery blond, through

reddish brown to black. Lions living at high altitudes and in colder climates tend to grow larger and darker manes than those living in warmer territories. Lions in captivity also tend to have longer manes than those in the wild.

At one time the lion was known through much of Europe, Africa and western Asia but today it is limited to central Africa, the Kruger Park in South Africa and the Gir forest sanctuary (an area of less than 500 square miles) in north-west India. Lions prefer open or lightly wooded grassland and rarely make their homes in thick forest, though they will live in semi-desert scrub and at heights of up to 10,000 feet above sea level.

Left and bottom Cougar, also known as panther, puma and mountain lion. The larger subspecies of cougar live in colder climates
Below The jaguarondi is the most weasel-like of the cats

Right Cougar. **Below** European wild cat

Lions do not display the same degree of territorial possessiveness as many other carnivores, although they tend to keep to a home range. They are highly sociable and are rarely seen alone. Unlike other cats, they live and hunt in groups, called prides, which will probably be a family party of an older male, several females of various ages, adolescent males and cubs. In thick bush country the pride will not usually number more than seven or eight beasts altogether, but where the terrain is open, it may include as many as thirty individuals. When very old or seriously injured and unable to play its part within the pride, a lion has to face a solitary existence and an unbalanced struggle to maintain himself.

Lions generally prey on the larger species of herbivorous animals, excluding adult pachyderms (elephant, hippopotamus and rhinoceros; young hippo and elephant have been taken on occasion), though old and injured animals will prey on smaller mammals, rodents and birds. Some species – zebra, wildebeest, waterbuck, impala and other antelopes for instance – may be favored in a particular district and the lion's

Top Lions are sociable animals. **Above** Ocelot

29

choice does not seem to be related to the abundance of a particular species in the area, so it is not simply a matter of one animal being more plentiful and therefore easier to find and kill. Lions are comparatively lazy animals and they do not hunt unless they are hungry. It has been estimated that on average they kill less than twice per month per beast—but with a large pride of thirty this would still mean frequent kills to keep them all adequately fed. Hunting is a community effort but the kill is more frequently made by a lioness.

Cubs are born in litters of two to four, or sometimes up to six after a gestation period of nearly twelve weeks. They are carefully nursed and stay with their mother until they are a year-and-a-half or more.

The young animals have a much more woolly coat than adults and are born with dark spots and stripes that fade as they mature. They remain longest on the legs and flanks and persist through adulthood in some individuals, usually lionesses. Lions are not fully mature until they are three years old and, because cubs are often the last to eat, in times of hardship mortality is high, particularly for males under two years.

Below A Kenyan lion. Only male lions have the majestic mane. **Bottom** Lioness and cubs in London Zoo. Lions are the easiest of the big cats to breed in captivity

Below and bottom Lion cubs in Nairobi
National Park. **Right** Track made by a lion

Opposite page A black-maned lion in the Ngorongoro crater, Tanzania, **Top** Lion in Amboseli National Park. **Above** Serengeti lioness. She clearly retains her juvenile spots **Right** Lioness

Tiger

Panthera tigris

The tiger is the largest member of the cat family and the giant Siberian tiger may measure over thirteen feet from nose to tip of tail and weigh as much as 650 pounds. A more average size would be just over nine feet long including three feet of tail, four to five hundred pounds in weight, and stand over three feet at the shoulder. Females are about a foot shorter and one hundred pounds lighter than equivalent males.

The ground color of the tiger's coat ranges from a yellowish fawn to an orange red—in some cases it may even be white—and is paler on the throat, belly and inside of the legs. It is always overlaid by black or very dark brown stripes running vertically over the head and body and horizontally around the legs. They frequently join to form a line running down the center of the forehead with whorls upon the cheeks and by the eyes. Sometimes the stripes are looped and broken into spots and only in the rare royal Bengal tiger are they actually unbroken black stripes. There are always bold white flashes, ringed with black, on the backs of the ears and there is a white spot over each eye. Tigers from the colder climates of Siberia and Manchuria have a winter coat consisting of thick under-fur and coarser outer hair five inches long. In most races, the cheek fur of adult males grows into a distinct ruff.

The tiger once ranged right across Asia, but its territory has now greatly contracted and most of its races are reduced to comparatively small numbers. Nevertheless it can still be found in terrain and climates as varied as the humid jungles from India to Java and in the forests of the cold and rocky mountains of Siberia and northern China.

Tigers are nocturnal hunters, especially where there is a lot of human activity, but they do hunt by day in conditions such as the jungles of Malaya, where they are shaded from direct sunlight, rarely troubled by humans and find their favorite prey, wild pig, readily available. Pig are a favorite prey throughout the tiger's range, followed by deer and antelopes, but they will eat a wide range of animals including monkeys, porcupines (whose spines make them a dangerous delicacy, for they can cause serious wounds), turtles, fish, locusts, young elephants and buffalo. Older tigers in particular prey on domestic livestock, for as they become heavy

The tiger is the largest of the big cats

and their teeth and claws less sharp, they find cattle an easy kill. In Nepal, for instance, older tigers used to leave the forests for open grassland where grazing cattle provided an easily available food supply. Nevertheless, there is evidence that in some parts of India tigers have left forested areas where game animals have disappeared, although there was still plenty of cattle about.

A tiger may eat up to fifty pounds of meat in a night but kills may be well spaced out. The average adult tiger claims about thirty victims every year with a total weight of around 6000 pounds. The Indian tiger is also reported to eat fruit, in particular that of the *Careya aborea* tree.

Tigers cannot climb well but are good swimmers. They have been known to swim out to take prey stranded by flood, and during excessively hot periods they may lie in shallow water to keep cool.

It is generally considered that tigers live and hunt alone except when mating, but there have been many reports of Indian tigers hunting in pairs and in Manchuria and Korea groups and families have been reported.

Tiger cubs are born in litters of three or four, occasionally as many as six, after a gestation period of about fifteen to sixteen weeks. It is rare for more than two of the litter to survive to maturity and they stay with their mother until they are two years old. They are born with the same markings as an adult.

Above and below Leopards are agile climbers
Opposite page Tiger

Leopard

Panthera pardus

The leopard is the third largest of the big cats, after the lion and the tiger. Leopards may be up to eight feet in length but more usual is about seven-and-a-half feet, the last three feet being tail. Their long body is carried on comparatively short legs and they stand about twenty-eight inches at the shoulder. A large male may weigh from 100 to 150 pounds and a female about 75 pounds. Their coat is dense and soft with rather short hair. The tawny yellow ground color becomes white on the underparts and the inside of the legs and is covered with black spots arranged in the form of rosettes, which are dense on the body and slightly less dense beneath. The back of the ears is black with a white spot. In heavily-wooded country leopards tend to be darker and smaller in size. Sometimes they are black all over; these individuals were once thought to be a separate species and known as black panthers, but they are only a variation and may occur in the same litter as normal spotted cubs. Black leopards still have the characteristic spots but they are difficult to see.

This cat has a wider geographical distribution than any other member of the cat family. It is found over most of Africa south of the Sahara, across Asia from Arabia and the Caucasus to China and Korea, in Ceylon, Sumatra and Java. In prehistoric times it ranged even farther through the Old World and fossils have been found in England. Leopards will live wherever sufficient cover is available, in forest, scrubland, open bush or rocky mountain slopes. They are fierce and powerful animals. Good climbers, they have been known to carry carcases as heavy as 150 pounds twelve to twenty feet up a tree away from other predators.

They prey on almost anything from antelopes to rodents, hares, frogs—even dung beetles!—and around the Kariba Lake of Zambia and Rhodesia they catch fish. Their great strength enables them to tackle animals bigger than themselves. Groups of up to six have occasionally been reported but they usually hunt alone, in the early morning, the evening and at night. Where they are hunted by man they are almost entirely nocturnal and lie up all through the day. A favorite hunting technique is to lie on a tree branch, well camouflaged by their spots against the dappled leaves, and drop upon prey as it passes underneath. Because they prey upon baboons, cave rats and other animals that destroy crops, they well outweigh in this way the damage they do by their occasional attacks on domestic livestock.

Cubs are born in litters of up to six but more usually of three, after a gestation period of about fifteen weeks. Their fur is dark and woolly with the spots close together and difficult to distinguish.

The black leopard, or black panther, is a color variation of the same species. Black leopards still retain their spots but they are difficult to distinguish

38

Snow leopard
Panthera uncia

The snow leopard, also known as the ounce, is closely related to the common leopard. It reaches seven feet or more from nose to tail tip, three feet of which is tail, and weighs up to ninety-five pounds.

The coat of thick hair is almost woolly and grows to about two inches long on the back and twice that length on the underparts. Its pale gray or gray-brown ground color may sometimes have a yellowish tinge but the underparts are pure white. Markings consist of large irregular black rosettes which form a black streak down the middle of the back.

Its range stretches from the Himalaya into the Hindu Kush and across Tibet as far as the north-east of Tsinghai and the west of Szechwan provinces in China and the Altai mountains. The snow leopard lives near the snow line and needs its thick coat to protect it from the cold. It follows its prey through the rocky grasslands between the snow line and the tree line and in summer up to pastures as much as 13,000 feet above sea level.

It lives on wild goats and sheep, boar, mush deer, Persian gazelle and small mammals, and hunts usually at night or late evening.

Litters of two to four are born in spring after a gestation period of about thirteen weeks and stay with their mother until they are about a year old.

The snow leopard, also known as the ounce, has been heavily hunted for its fur

Jaguar
Panthera onca

Male jaguar

The jaguar is the largest of the cat family in the New World, and about the same size as the Old World leopard. They average a little over eight feet long when fully grown including a relatively short tail of two to two-and-a-half feet length and stand about twenty-eight inches at the shoulder. They are big boned and their heavy chest, considerable girth and powerfully muscled forelegs make even female jaguars heavier and more powerful than male pumas and considerably heavier than the African leopard. In the Amazon basin and on the upper Paraguay they reach weights of 250 pounds and in northern Peru they have been recorded well over 300 pounds, though in Mexico they are much lighter and smaller.

The coat consists of short, rather bristly fur which varies from a yellow to a tawny ground color with a whitish belly. It is overlaid with black or very dark brown spots grouped in rosettes, which have further spots within them, or solid blotches, which particularly occur along the spine and on the limbs, while the tail is ringed towards its tip. The face is spotted and the backs of the ears are black, but the jaguar does not have the white flash behind the ear which occurs in many other cats. There is a great deal of variation in the actual markings—the rosettes sometimes assume an almost rectangular shape. They are fewer and usually larger than on the leopard but the two cats' pelts are sometimes confused—though not in the wild, since they have separate existences in two different hemispheres.

As with several other cats, coloration seems to be darker among jaguars from heavily forested regions. Black jaguars are frequent and much more common than among other big cats. As with panthers, this is a 'melanistic' variation not a separate race, and black jaguars occur in the same litter as spotted cubs. It does not seem to be related to environment for many black jaguars occur in the dry tablelands of northeastern Brazil.

The jaguar is the largest of the American big cats

The jaguar's range is even wider than that of the cougar. Its northern limit extends from southern California across Arizona to where the Colorado empties into the Gulf of Mexico, and it can be found as far south as the pampas of Argentina and the Rio Negro. Its territory is defined more by the presence of suitable prey than by any climatic conditions, for it can be found equally in the mangrove swamps of the west coast of Mexico, the steaming jungle of the Amazon, high in the Andes of Peru and Bolivia, on the dry pampas of the Argentine and in the near-desert of central Mexico and California.

The jaguar is usually a solitary hunter and despite some reports of small prides in more remote areas, it appears to be gregarious only at breeding time, when groups of eight or more have been seen. In areas where it has been hunted by man, the jaguar hunts almost exclusively at night and lies up most of the day, sometimes making its den in the ruins of the ancient civilizations of Central and South America. Its prey will vary according to the fauna of the terrain but includes deer, agoutis,

tapirs and, in particular, the pig-like peccaries. The jaguar is a fine swimmer and likes water, so an easier prey is the capybara, a large guinea-pig-like rodent that lives on the banks of lakes and rivers. It is also an agile climber and will take monkeys and other tree living animals, sometimes jumping down on them from above. However, the jaguar's weight prevents it from climbing out on higher branches so sloths and monkeys that can climb high will keep out of reach. The jaguar also catches fish.

Cubs are born in litters of up to four after a gestation period of about fourteen weeks. They have a long woolly coat, heavily marked with spots. In the tropical forests the jaguar appears to breed at any time of year but at the edges of their range, in the southern United States and the Argentine pampas, it produces its young in the early spring.

Clouded leopard

Neofelis nebulosa

Despite its name, the clouded leopard is not a close relation of the leopard proper. An adult may range from a little over two feet to three-foot-six plus two to three feet of tail, and weigh from twenty-four to nearly fifty pounds.

The ground color of the coat is greenish yellow, darkening to yellowish brown on the flanks, and the dark markings vary considerably, consisting of circles, rosettes, blotches and ovals with dashes and spots on the limbs and head and broken rings on the tail. There are usually two deep black lines down the back and large black rosettes on the flanks, with spots and dots in the centers. Two sets of semicircular black and white marks enclose a dark patch on the forehead.

It lives in thick jungle, shrub and even swamps, from Nepal eastwards to the south of China and Taiwan and south to Borneo, Java and Sumatra. It climbs well, using its long heavy tail to help its balance, and sleeps off the ground if possible. During the day it rests in trees, descending (sometimes in daytime) to hunt birds, monkeys, goats, pigs and deer.

It falls somewhere between the two genera *Felis* and *Panthera*, and has been placed by zoologists in a genus of its own. Because it is largely nocturnal and very shy, little is known of its habits.

Domestic cat

Felis catus

The usual domesticated cat, varies through numerous breeds, but all belong to the same species. They may have evolved from a crossing of *Felis libyca* with *Felis sylvestris* but zoologists are not agreed on this.

The pet cat has all the characteristics of its larger relations, except for the acceptance of a close relationship with man. If one studies a domestic cat's behavior with its kittens and with other animals, one will observe much that mirrors the life of the big cats in miniature.

The markings of the clouded leopard are totally unlike those of the leopard

Species in danger

Slow but wide-ranging changes in the earth's climate, and the unbalancing of the ecology by the too-successful hunting of a form of prey, had their influence in the past on the survival and distribution of the carnivores. But since the arrival of man on the scene, his activities have outweighed all else. Some species have been exterminated by the hunter, but more important have been the changes brought about by felling forests, clearing ground, raising crops and making first claim on the world's resources.

When the great ice sheets retreated at the end of the Ice Ages there were lions in the caves of Britain and lynx in the forests. After so long a time, it is no great shock to find that they have disappeared, but in our own times the change has been rapid, and catastrophic. The typical race of lion, *Panthera leo leo*, a native of Africa north of the Sahara, the lion most known to Europeans and from which the species was described, *is now extinct*, and has been since 1922. In India the only lions left are limited to one small area and are seriously threatened by human pressures.

The lion retreated gradually through Europe and became increasingly rare in southern Europe until by 100 AD there were thought to be no native lions remaining. In North Africa and Asia the increase in human population and human needs, coupled with hunting to defend livestock and the improvement of weapons hastened the extinction of the North African lion. In southern Africa, hunting for sport and to defend cattle led similarly to the extermination of the Cape lion, *Felis leo metanochaitus*, so that only the lions of Asia and of Central and East Africa are left today. The tiger's range has retracted from a wide area of Asia, which once included Japan.

The cats of North America fell before the firearms of frontiersmen and farmers or were trapped for their furs. The lynx, for instance, was valued for its pelt and helped to fill the coffers of the Hudson's Bay Company from the earliest days of Canada's colonization. Even more effective in reducing its numbers was the development of forestry. In Europe it was driven farther and farther north until, in Sweden, its one-time northern limit became its southern one, creating sterner conditions under which to find food or rear young. It is believed to have been reduced to only a score or so of animals. In 1928, the Swedish government made the lynx a protected animal and since then it has increased its numbers in Scandinavia and begun to move south. The Spanish lynx (*lynx pardina*) has maintained a hold in parts of Spain, especially the Donana reserve.

If the existing members of the cat family are to survive it will be because man decides to stop the destruction of their habitat, give up the killing of animals for their skins and become, in all senses, a conservationist. Meanwhile, there is a number of species or subspecies which are particularly threatened.

The International Union for the Conservation of Nature and Natural Resources keeps a record – their famous *Red Data Book* – of surviving species now in danger of extinction. These are the big cats that appear in that list:

The Asiatic lion

Panthera leo persica

At the beginning of the twentieth century, there were still lions in the more remote parts of Arabia, but none now survive, and although they were still known along the upper waters of the Euphrates only a century ago they had all disappeared by 1920. In Iraq, the last specimens were captured before 1914. In Iran, they were thought extinct before the Second World War, but two sightings of lions were reported in 1941 and it is just possible that some may survive in the mountainous country of south-western Iran. In Pakistan no lions have been known since 1842, and in most of India the last free lion was killed in 1884. This lion now survives only in the 500 square miles of the Gir forest in the south-western corner of the Kathiawar peninsular. Here, in 1900, the only lions remaining of those which had ranged the Punjab, Bengal and

Baroda were brought under the protection of the local prince, the Nawab of Junagardh and declared a protected animal. (The Nawab retained the right for a limited number to be shot by his guests). In 1966, the forest became the Gir Wild Life Sanctuary.

From less than 100 lions at the turn of the century, the population had increased to 289 in 1936 and in 1963 there were 285; but in 1968 only about 162. The census was made by counting the number of lion kills over a month, making a tally of pug-marks over two days, and placing 100 buffalo calves throughout the forest, on the assumption that within a couple of days pretty well all the lions would have found a bait and would stay near it while the count was made. Totals for the three methods were then compared –they came to 160, 166 and 162. Of course, a few lions may have missed the count.

The forest consists of only about 50% timber, the rest being scrub and secondary growths which are constantly damaged by browsing animals and indiscriminately hacked by their owners. Beyond the timber, the territory ranges from thorn scrub to dense thickets of acacia, barren earth and pockets of cultivation. During the dry season there is little cover for the wild-life apart from the growths along the banks of the rivers and streams. These flood during the wet season and new growths appear in otherwise barren areas beyond the forest, providing fresh grazing for domestic cattle, which in turn attract the lions from their usual territories. Over 7000 humans and about eight times that number of domestic animals live in the forest. Half that number of buffalo, cattle, goats and camels could graze the forest without damage but 100% overgrazing has destroyed the undergrowth and

Asiatic lion, lioness and lioness with cubs in the Gir Forest, India, the only place where the species has survived in the wild

the young trees. The forest is being killed, giving place first to thorn scrub, then to desert.

The available food and cover grows less and less, the wild animals on which the lions prey can no longer survive. The lions consequently kill ten to twenty domestic animals each day, which the cattle owners seem to tolerate. Since the herdsmen are Hindu they do not slaughter their cattle and the depredations of the lions are the only limiting factor. A culling of less than six thousand beasts a year out of nearly sixty thousand cannot stop the destructive process and, unless some way can be found of persuading the cattle owners to accept strict controls and a big reduction in the number of stock, in twenty years there will be no forest to support cattle, humans or lions.

In 1957, three lions were taken from the Gir forest to the Chandraprabha Sanctuary in Uttar Pradesh, where they have bred and appear to flourish. In this way the Asian lion may be preserved by transferring breeding colonies to other sanctuaries. In the Gir itself, the situation is improving; a new captive breeding nucleus is being established just outside the forest, with the specific aim of putting the progeny back into the sanctuary. Real efforts to resettle the local people living within its boundaries are reported to have begun.

The Caspian tiger
Panthera tigris virgata
This small to medium-sized race with dark coloring once ranged from Georgia and Armenia to lake Balkash and into China, across the north of Afghanistan and as far as the Altai mountains and the Irtysh valley in the north. In more recent times the range has contracted to the north. Although there were one or two isolated sightings up to 1951, it seems likely that there are now no tigers of this race in the USSR and that the remaining population is limited to not more than a score of tigers in northern Iran near the shores of the Caspian Sea and others, perhaps a larger number, in northern Afghanistan, some of whom occasionally wander northwards into Soviet Azerbaijan and Tadzhikistan.

The reduction of the tigers east of the Caspian has been partly due to hunting and partly to the clearing of its natural cover to grow cotton. In Iran the destruction of forest cover and the increase in human activity following control of the malaria mosquito on the Caspian coast have been largely responsible for the decline in the tiger population. Illegal hunting for highly-valued skins has added to their danger. A wildlife sanctuary has been established in northeastern Iran, but it is not known how many tigers live within its territory. In the USSR, tigers are fully protected and several hundred are claimed to live within its borders. It is possible that wandering specimens may become established there, but since the tiger is such a traveler it may range outside the areas where it is protected and be destroyed.

Amur or Siberian tiger
Panthera tigris altaica
This long-haired tiger, the largest race of the species, once ranged through the snows and forests of Siberia from the upper waters of the Lena river to lake Baikal in the west, through the valleys of the Amur river and its tributaries to the east, and south to eastern Mongolia, Korea and China as far as the Hwang Ho. Now it is limited to the mountains of north Korea (40–45 tigers), the northern provinces of Manchuria and the extreme east of Siberia in the Sikhote Alin mountains, north of Vladivostok. Here the tigers are protected by law and two large wildlife reserves have been established. To discourage them from killing domestic cattle, attempts have been made to increase the wild boar population, as they would form a large part of the tiger's natural prey. Nevertheless, there are indications that the number of tigers seriously declined during the 1960s.

Amur, or Siberian tigers in San Diego Zoo

Chinese tiger
Panthera tigris amoyensis

This race originally ranged from as far north as Peking, through south and eastern China and up the river valleys of the west into the provinces of Kansu and Szechwan. Today, the western range is much more limited and, since the tiger is considered a danger to human life and so not protected, it is still hunted and survives only in isolated populations.

Sumatran tiger
Panthera tigris sumatrae

This small tiger formerly florished in the north and mountainous south-west of Sumatra, but hunting and trapping, particularly in the last twenty years, have reduced its population to a dangerously low number.

Javan tiger
Panthera tigris sondaica

Once numerous in many parts of Java, this race has been hunted almost to extinction. Although shooting permits have officially been required in Java since 1940, it is now reduced to four or five small populations in the east of the island. Recent estimates gave five animals in the Betiri Reserve and recorded the extinction of tigers in the Udjong Kulon Reserve in western Java, where nine animals lived in the late 1960s.

Bali tiger
Panthera tigris balica

This race is now differentiated from the Javan population, but it has been suggested that it was originally introduced from Java by man. Tigers were once widespread over all except the eastern end of the island but no sighting has been reported since 1953. Hunters from Java still seek any specimens that may exist but it is possible that this race is already extinct.

Indian or Bengal tiger
Panthera tigris tigris

This race has recently been included in the *Red Data Book*, and the Indian government, with the help of the World Wildlife Fund and the IUCN, is establishing a number of reserves specifically for the Bengal tiger, in an all-out effort to save it from extinction.

Sumatran tiger at Whipsnade

Barbary leopard
Panthera pardus panthera

The range of this large leopard includes Morocco, Algeria and Tunisia, and even half a century ago it was still comparatively common in suitable terrain. Now it can be found only in two areas: the Central Atlas mountains and in the forests of the Oulms region. Until recently it still survived in the Akfadou National Park in Algeria and possibly in parts of Tunisia in the mountains of Tamerza and the forests between Bizerta and Tabarka, but it is now presumed extinct in both countries. Cultivation and the increase of grazing herds reduced the leopard's natural prey and encouraged it to prey on domestic cattle, thereby inviting its slaughter by herdsmen, but in recent years the price fetched by its valuable fur has been a more important factor leading to its destruction.

Sinai leopard
Panthera pardus jarvisi

Once established in Sinai and northern Saudi Arabia, this race is now extremely rare and may prove to be extinct.

Arabian leopard
Panthera pardus nimr

This race ranges from the southern part of the Arabian peninsular to the Yemen and Oman, but heavy hunting has now made it extremely rare.

Anatilian leopard
Panthera pardus tulliana

Once widespread throughout the west of Asia Minor and the transcaucasian Republics of the USSR, this race now survives in small numbers in Israel, Turkey and possibly in Syria and Jordan also, but is extinct in the Caucasus. Attempts are being made to preserve it in Turkey, particularly in Kusadasi National Park.

Amur leopard
Panthera pardus orientalis

This race ranged widely through Korea, Manchuria and the Primorskaya Oblast of the USSR, east of the Amur river but is now restricted to small populations in North Korea and close to Lake Khanka, north of Vladivostock.

Above The eastern cougar (see page 50)
Below Amur leopard in captivity

47

Snow leopard

Panthera uncia

Although it may once have ranged from the Himalayas and the Altai mountains as far as highland Iran, this species is now restricted to the central Asian highlands of China, India, Pakistan, Afghanistan and the USSR. Heavily hunted for its valuable fur, it used to be trapped in pits baited with sheep or goats. It is protected in the USSR, where it survives in the wildlife reserves of Zaamin in Uzbekhistan and Aksov-Djebogly in Kazakhstan, and in Pakistan and India (except Kashmir). The present population has been estimated at about 400, including not more than 250 in the Himalaya.

Formosan clouded leopard

Neofelis nebulosa brachyurus

This subspecies is distinguished by the paleness of its fur, shortish tail (about twenty inches) and rather indistinct black banding. It has been reduced to a dangerous level by uncontrolled hunting for its highly-valued fur.

Barbary serval

Felis serval constantina

This is now isolated in distribution, living only in the humid forest zones of Algeria. It has a long full coat.

Asiatic cheetah

Acinonyx jubatus venaticus

Ranged through Israel and Arabia to Turkmenistan, Afghanistan, Baluchistan and northern India, until destruction of its habitat and reduction of its prey, together with persistent hunting, exterminated the population in India by 1950 and in Israel more than a hundred years ago. It is probably also extinct in Jordan and survives only in Turkmenistan, Kazakhstan, Afghanistan, south-west Iran and possibly in Baluchistan, northern Saudi Arabia and Oman.

Florida cougar

Felis concolor coryi

This race, which can be up to seven feet long, with brighter coloring and smaller feet than some of the other subspecies, used to range westwards from Florida and the south of Southern Carolina to the far side of the Mississippi valley in Louisiana and Arkansas. The decrease in the deer population due to human expansion has restricted the food supply, and in many parts of the USA the cougar has taken to killing domestic cattle and young horses. In return, all races have been savagely hunted with dogs and guns and the species exterminated almost everywhere east of the Mississippi. At one time, the Florida subspecies was thought to be extinct but it has survived in the Everglades and shows signs of re-establishing itself within the protected area of the Everglades National Park.

Above left Snow leopard at London Zoo. **Left** Spoor of a snow leopard at 14,000 feet in Nepal **Opposite page above** Black leopard. **Below** Leopard

Eastern cougar

Felis concolor cougar

This race, which ranged from the south-eastern states of the USA through to Canada and westward to the plains, was extinct in the USA by 1900 and exceedingly rare in Canada. It is now believed to be increasing in number and extending its territories, since forest exploitation has created ideal conditions for the grouse and deer on which the cougar preys.

Spanish lynx

Felis lynx pardina

The Spanish lynx once ranged over most of the suitable terrain in Spain and Portugal and it is possible that it still survives in isolated places in the Pyrenees, though there is some doubt as to whether any surviving Pyrenean population belong to this race or to that of the northern lynx. The clearing of the woodland that forms the lynx's natural habitat and hunting to prevent its attacks on domestic animals have exterminated it in the rest of the Iberian peninsula, except for small areas where hunting has been controlled in the Guadalquivir peninsula. Here, the establishment of the Coto Donana nature reserve in 1965 will protect the lynx, for

Spanish lynx in the Coto Donana zoo

although there is nothing to prevent its being hunted elsewhere–and it is still on the list of destructive animals which can be shot at any time–it will be safe within its borders.

There are no South American felines currently listed as in danger, but the ocelots, margays and jaguars of the Americas are highly prized for their skins and are ruthlessly hunted. Their numbers are plummetting badly. Ian Grimwood, Technical Wildlife Adviser to the Peruvian government, gave the following figures for skins traded at Iquitos in the upper Amazon in

1966: *ocelots* 15,000; *margays and tiger cats* 4000; *jaguars* 891. United States import figures showed that for the first *eight months* of 1968, 7238 jaguar skins were imported into the USA. These animals are in increasing danger of extinction. The United States have recently banned the importation of their skins, and it is to be hoped that the British government will soon do the same.

It was realized long ago that the establishment of game reserves and the limitation of hunting were not enough. Now several governments have banned the killing of certain endangered species–tigers, for instance, can no longer be shot in Pakistan or Bangladesh. Others have controlled the traffic in animal skins. India banned the commercial export of tiger and leopard skins in 1968, and in 1970 stopped their personal export by tourists. But measures like this may mean that the trade simply moves elsewhere. Prior to the Indian ban of 1968, 3660 leopard skins were exported in one year to the United States alone. After the ban, the figure dropped to 895–but the figure for neighboring Nepal rose from 95 to 1773. Fortunately, Nepal banned both the import and export of skins in 1971.

When a single leopard skin may be worth more than a shepherd's yearly income (a statistic officially quoted by the Somali government), and very much more by the time the fur traders have taken their profit, the incentive to find a way of by-passing the law is enormous. One way of combating this is to make sure that there is no market for the skins. In the USA, federal law now prevents the import of animals or articles made from animals on the Red Book list, and from the ocelot, jaguar, margay and tiger cat. However, since it is difficult to prove that the skin belongs to the actual subspecies on the endangered list even endangered species could still be imported under another name.

In 1970, New York State took a further step by banning both import and sale of *all* species of leopard, cheetah, jaguar and tiger, but this was challenged by a footwear company and the courts ruled that it was unconstitutional and limited the ban to those animals included in the federal lists.

In 1972, Great Britain introduced legislation which prohibits the import of 'furs, skins, rugs and coverlets obtained from the tiger and the snow and clouded leopards'. It also strengthened the regulations for the import of cheetah and leopard skins which require certificates to show that they were legally killed or exported. But this legislation still allows the importing of made-up articles such as fur coats and handbags and it is not, therefore, as effective as it ought to be.

But is the action that is being taken to ensure that more animals do not disappear for ever enough? It is sadly obvious that it is not. What can be done to help? We can all at least add our own voices to the demand that animals shall not be slaughtered wholesale for their skins and if we have the means we can give practical financial support to the organizations seeking to defend the world that human beings have so ruthlessly exploited. These are some of the addresses of the World Wildlife Fund to which contributions can be sent:

United States of America
World Wildlife Fund Inc.
Suite 619
910 17th Street NW
Washington, DC 20006

Canada
World Wildlife Fund of Canada
40 St. Clair Avenue West
Suite 300
Toronto 7

United Kingdom
British National Appeal
World Wildlife Fund
7–8 Plumtree Court
London EC4A 4DN

South Africa
South African Wildlife Foundation
Die SA Natuurstigting
PO Box 456
Stellenbosch

How the leopard got his spots

A fable from Sierra Leone

One day the leopard met the fire burning quietly in a clearing, and they became very friendly. The leopard used to go to see the fire every day but the fire never returned his visit. The leopard's wife was annoyed that he spent so much time away from home with his friend and told him that it was not much of a friend who let the leopard make the journey to see him every day but could never make the effort to come and visit them in return. The fire must be too proud to visit them and think their home too lowly for such as he–how could her husband make a friend of someone like that?

The leopard told the fire that his wife wondered why he never came to visit and begged him to pay a call on them. At first the fire made excuses, saying that he never visited anyone. Eventually he agreed, but explained that he never walked and it would only be possible to come if there was a path of dry leaves from his home to the leopard's door.

The leopard was very pleased that the fire was going to visit them and told his wife to gather leaves. They made their home ready to entertain their special guest and laid a path of dry leaves from the fire's home right up to their house and waited for their visitor. Soon they heard loud crackling and the rush of a strong wind outside the door and the leopard went to see what was the matter. It was the fire come to visit. He reached out his fiery fingers and the flames touched the leopard and his wife. They were so frightened that they jumped backwards out of the window. Already the flames had spread into the house and in only a few moments it had burned down. The leopard never asked the fire to visit again and to this day he and his wife have black marks all over their bodies where the fire touched them.

Kittens and cubs. **Opposite page top** Lions
Middle left Northern lynx. **Bottom left**
Leopard. **Top** Lions. **Left** Servals. **Above** Bobcat

Opposite page A lion killed in the royal hunt shown in the Nineveh palace reliefs. The stylized treatment of the mane is typical of these Assyrian carvings. **Above** The lion avenue on the sacred island of Delos. Greeks, Egyptians and other ancient peoples carved lions to guard the approaches to their temples

Gods of the jungle and mountain

The Sphinx, erected nearly five thousand years ago at the foot of the great pyramids of Gizeh, has the body of a lion and the head of the early pharaoh Khephren. It is the symbol of the rising sun and of resurrection for the pharaoh whose tomb it guards. But to the Egyptians, the lion was much more than a symbol, it was a shape in which many of their most powerful gods appeared. It was one of the original forms in which the sun-god was depicted, the god who appeared as Horus in the morning and as Ra in the afternoon (Ra later being sometimes represented as a hawk-headed lion). It was a shape which might be taken by the three daughters of the sun: Tefenet, Sekhmet and Bast (Bast later becoming identified with the domestic cat).

To people brought up with the simplified and monotheistic religions of today, the continual change of form and name, and the overlapping of responsibilities and powers, among the gods of ancient Egypt makes their pantheon appear most confusing, but its inconsistencies did not occur to the people who worshipped them. Among the lesser gods, the lioness Men'et was the nurse of Horus; a grim-looking lion called Mihos was worshipped as the son of Ra and Bast in Upper Egypt; the lioness Mehet was worshipped in the city of This, while at Heliopolis they had a lion-headed goddess known as Menehtet.

The south wind was represented with the head or body of a lion, in reference to its burning character, and there are pictures on monuments from prehistoric times, and on the magic wands of the Middle Kingdom, showing a strange lion or leopard god of unknown name with a long and twisting neck.

Aker, the early god of the earth, was depicted as a lion with two heads. It was believed that at night, when the disc of the sun disappeared behind the mountains of the west, it had been swallowed by one of Aker's heads and passed inside his body—that is, through the earth— until at morning it came out through his other mouth and appeared over the mountains of the east. When another god, called Geb, became more widely venerated as the god of the earth, Aker became associated with the underworld and death and was depicted as a black

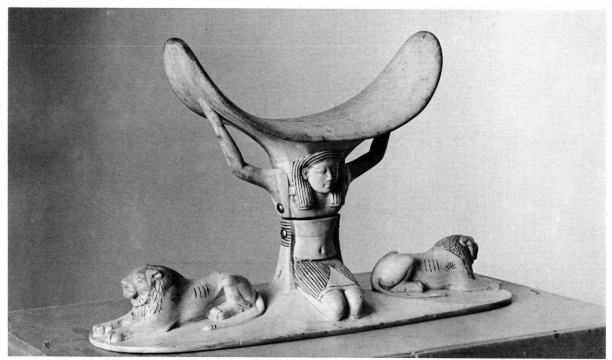

A headrest from the tomb of Tutankhamun shows Shu in human form with two lions representing the mountains of the eastern and western horizons—the symbols for yesterday and tomorrow. The significance of the rosettes on their shoulders is unknown. They may represent ornaments placed on live tame lions

lion. Later still, the form was changed into that of two lions lying back to back and either carrying or representing the mountains of the morning and the evening, so that they became known as the symbols for yesterday and tomorrow. These double lions also became confused with the 'celestial lions,' the goddess Tefenet and her brother-husband Shu, who were the gods of the air and the æthereal space which separates the sky (Shu's daughter Nut) from the earth (his son Geb).

Often, as in the illustration on this page, the lion god Shu is represented in a human form and without his sister-wife. His cult-center was called in Greek *Leonopolis*, and at his temple there a real lion was kept and tended reverently as his representative.

Sekhmet was the terrible goddess of war and battle. Her name, which means 'the powerful', is one of the titles of the great goddess Hathor who is usually presented as a cow or with a cow's attributes.

The leopard also played a role in Egyptian religion. Sekhanit, the goddess responsible for writing, is always depicted wearing a leopard skin and this became the regular vestment worn by all Egyptian priests. In Tutankhamun's tomb, a wooden figure of the dead pharaoh shows him standing poised upon the back of a partly gilded leopard. The purpose of the figure is unknown, but wooden leopards with mortices cut in their backs, presumably to carry similar statuettes, were found in three other tombs of the eighteenth Dynasty. In another tomb, a wall painting shows the statuette of a pharaoh carried on the back of a lion. It can be deduced that the big cats played some role in conducting the dead kings to the underworld.

Moving across to Asia, the lion's religious symbolism persists. In Babylon there was Nergal, god of the underworld, who, like Aker, took a leonine form. In Assyria, the lion, often with wings and a human head, stands sphinx-like as a guardian to keep devils and evil influences from entering the gates of palaces.

The goddess Sekhmet who, in lion form, set about the slaughter of the human race

The pharaoh Tutankhamun on a leopard's back. Similar leopard figures, and one of a lion carrying a statuette of a king, have been found in other tombs. The big cats probably played a role in carrying the dead king through the underworld

Huge and magnificent carved lions flanked the great temple of Ishtar, built at Nimrod in 880 BC. Ishtar was the great mother-goddess of Mesopotamia. She was responsible for the fertility of the earth and for sexuality, and appears in varied forms as Astarte and Qodshu in other parts of the Middle East. In Assyria, she became the powerful goddess of war and was closely associated with the national god Ashur. She is described in inscriptions as 'perfect in courage'. She traveled in a chariot drawn by seven lions and is often depicted standing on a lion's back.

Farther east, in China, the lion is still considered to have power. Although China is well beyond the lion's range and the ancient Chinese are unlikely ever to have seen a lion, they still stand guard at temples and imperial palaces, sometimes transformed into the imperial

lion-dog—which we know as the Pekinese. But the great feline god in the east is the tiger. The white tiger, Bach-ho, was the spirit of the west, and Ta-sheng, the Guardian or Great Spirit, was often painted in tiger forms on the walls of houses.

The primitive Gonds in India worshipped a tiger god which represented the spirit of the wild. They built a house for him in the forest and believed that in the form of a great white tiger he would chase away any other beasts who harassed their livestock or themselves. In many other countries, the tiger is treated with respect and not killed. In Sumatra, for instance, the people have been known to go where Europeans have set traps and explain to any tigers that may be able to hear that *they* are not responsible. If they have to kill a man-eater for their own protection, they first try to catch him so that they can explain how sorry they are that his behavior makes it necessary for them to end his life, and ask his forgiveness before they kill him.

It was in the Americas that the big cat gods achieved their highest standing. In the ancient civilizations of Mexico and Peru, and in the complex mythology of the Indian tribes, jaguar, puma and ocelot exerted a supernatural influence.

The complex religious beliefs and customs of the Olmecs, the Toltecs, the Zapotecs, the Maya, the Aztecs, the Incas and the other cultures of Pre-Columbian America are difficult to interpret and still incompletely understood. The exact functions of the feline gods are not known, and in different cultures at different times, various gods held the same or overlapping

60

Opposite page Tiger painted on a wall in Udaipur, India, where it is a typical decoration on the houses—a reminder of the role the tiger has played in Asian folk-culture. **Above** Bengal tiger. **Right** Lion decoration on a railway carriage built for Queen Victoria. The lion mask has been used by sculptors and designers to embellish everything from a fountain to a coat-button

functions, but in all of them, the images of pumas, jaguars or ocelots appear in temple carvings, as masks and on ritual objects.

As a rough guide, in Mexico the jaguar seems to have held the same place in the mythology of the forested lowland as the ocelot held in grassy plateau country, while in Peru the jaguar appears in highland cultures and the puma among those of the southern coast. Jaguar carvings of the north Andean Chavin culture date back six thousand years. The Mayas gave the rain gods of the four quarters jaguar form and built a great temple of the jaguar at Tikal in Guatemala.

Like the lion of Africa, the jaguar was at first the symbol of the sun. The people of Mexico believed that he was struck by the club of the plumed serpent Quetzalcoatl and turned into a jaguar, the man-devouring demon of the night which could be seen high in the sky at night as the constellation which Europeans call the Great Bear.

Under the name Tezcatlipoca (Smoking Mirror) the jaguar became a moon god, lord of the underworld and of the dead. He was the patron of magicians and 'the dragon of the eclipse'.

Another jaguar, or perhaps a variant form of the same god, was Tepeyollotl (Heart of the Mountain), the god of Calli, third day of the month, with a role resembling that of the Egyptian Aker, for it was he who leaped from the cavern of the earth to seize the sun between his jaws as it descended in the west. Tepeyollotl had a terrible roar which might be heard in the evening echoing around the hills. It was the noise of thunder, of avalanches and volcanoes.

This god had the power to cause earthquakes and eruptions, and he himself becomes a form of the sun when underneath the earth at night.

In later Aztec hymns, the ocelot becomes the symbol of the sun by night (the eagle being his representative during the day). He is described as an underworld creature coming howling out of the night, bringing the rain for the sun to rise fresh each morning.

The fourteenth day of the month was the day of the ocelot, who was considered the bravest of animals. He (or the jaguar) was the protective spirit of the young warriors who acted as advance guards and scouts for the Aztec armies, spying out the land as keenly as he was thought to watch for the sun coming to devour the stars.

Left Bes, an Egyptian domestic god of pleasure, was often presented with a lion's attributes as in this ointment jar from Tutankhamun's tomb
Above This great carved lion used to guard the entrance to the temple of Ishtar at Nimrod

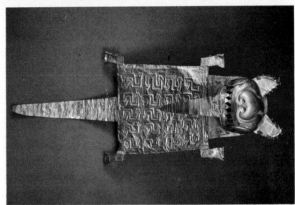

Above The tiger was the great god of the wild in eastern Asia. **Right** Cougar made in gold, 4th–9th century AD, by the Mohicas of Peru

The two noble warrior orders of Mexico were the Ocelot Knights and the Eagle Knights (who were the main assault troops) and their uniform made them look like their protectors. Aztec pictures show the Eagles covered in feathers with a great beaked headdress and the Ocelots apparently dressed in actual skins with their faces seen between the open jaws of the animal's mouth.

At Malinalco there is a circular temple with an entrance carved like a serpent's head with fangs and eyes and flanked by figures of Eagle and Ocelot Knights. Inside is a circular stone bench carved with eagles and an ocelot. It is probably a temple of the sun, to whose service the knightly orders took their vows. During the 'Month of the Skinning of Men,' when great numbers were sacrificed and then flayed, the priests who officiated were dressed as jaguars and ocelots.

In the primitive jungle tribes, the cat gods likewise held power. Offerings would be made to them, and many tribes claim a jaguar as their original ancestor. A jaguar's eye-teeth are used by the Chavante Indians to barb their arrows and many peoples wear a jaguar's teeth as a talisman. On the southern coast of Peru, the people who created the Paracas necropolis wove puma demons on the burial blankets of their dead. The Chibca tribes made pots to look like jaguars crouching to attack. Everywhere, from the great Mayan or Toltec jaguar throne found at Chichen Itzá (Yucatán), to the living superstitions of the Quintana Roo, where offerings to jaguar corn-gods are still tied to trees, the belief in the power of the big cats can be seen to be strong.

Tiri and the jaguars

A legend of the Yuracare people, who live in a remote part of Brazil, at the foot of the Andes. The story begins when a young woman, the daughter of the man who survived the great fire which is the Yuracare equivalent to the Bible story of the flood, found a beautiful tree in the forest.

The maiden was fascinated by the tree and wished that it was a young man so that she could give him her love. She painted it and decorated it and gave it all her attention. Magically it became transformed into a young man called Ule, and she was happy.

Her happiness was not to last; Ule was killed by a jaguar. Dutifully she collected all the pieces she could find and he was miraculously brought to life, but there was a piece missing. Walking past a pool one day, Ule looked at his reflection and saw his disfigured face where the piece was missing. He told the maiden that he must leave her and that she must walk on and not look behind whatever noise she heard. But she did look back, and though she saw no sign of her lover, she got lost and wandered into a jaguar's den, where a female and four cubs lived.

The mother jaguar took pity on her but the four sons were for killing her. If she were to live, she must be obedient to their wishes, and to test her obedience they commanded her to eat the poisonous ants that infested their bodies. She tricked them and instead of eating the ants substituted seeds which she spat out on the ground. Three of the jaguar cubs did not notice but the fourth had eyes in the back of his head, saw what she was doing and killed her. She was already carrying Ule's child and the jaguar mother knew this and tore the unborn baby from her body and cared for it herself. This baby was known as Tiri.

When Tiri was grown up, he wounded a paca, which complained to him: 'Why do you try to kill me, who have never done you any harm, when you live in peace with the murderers of your own mother?' When he knew what had happened, Tiri lay in wait for the jaguars. He took up his bow and arrows and slew three of them, but the fourth, the one with eyes in the back of his head, climbed a tree and called upon the trees, the sun, the moon and the stars to save him. The moon reached down and snatched him up and, since then, if you look at the moon when it is full you can see the jaguar lying in her arms.

Now Tiri was free of the four jaguars he became the lord of all nature and taught the arts of cultivation to the mother jaguar. Tiri's story continues until at last he leads human beings out into the world from a great rock and the earth becomes populated.

Above, right and opposite page above Jaguars and jaguar young. **Opposite page below** Jaguarundi catching a snake

Life in the wild

Most of the cat family lead solitary lives and like to keep well out of the way of human beings, making it difficult to study their habits. In the past, much of our information came from big game hunters and therefore we know that lions tend to be gregarious. Sightings of the other cats in groups, other than mother and cubs, are uncommon, and adult pairs are usually seen only at mating times. Bobcat males are said to help collect food once the kittens are weaned, and it is possible that some of the other smaller cats may maintain family pairings.

The tigress

Times of mating and gestation periods vary between the different species of cat (see *The Cat Family*), but even with the lion and tiger the cubs are only carried for 105–113 days. This is a short period for such a large mammal, but longer might create problems for a predator. Tiger cubs weigh about three pounds each at birth. Their eyes open within a week or fourteen days but they appear to stay short-sighted for several weeks. This prevents them from going far from their lair while their mother is away hunting. She will begin to wean them after about six weeks, giving them regurgitated pieces of part-digested meat, but she is still in milk until the cubs are five or six months old. Sometimes a tigress will take small animals with tender flesh back to the cubs but others will lead their family to the kill where the cubs can tackle meat which has already begun to decompose.

Left Cougar in Beaver Park, Colorado. **Above** Tiger cub. **Opposite page** A tiger's territory may range to several hundred square miles

This is probably the first stage in their hunting training – apart from chasing their mother's tail. Jim Corbett, author of *Maneaters of Kumaon*, has described a tigress leading her cubs up to a kill which she had hidden under a pile of leaves. The two small cubs followed carefully in her tracks, freezing when she stopped, avoiding every obstacle she avoided, and putting down and lifting up each paw with infinite care. Some thirty yards distant from the kill the tigress lay down. Somehow the cubs knew that the kill lay in the direction that their mother's nose was pointing and continued their careful way. The cubs passed very close to the smelly, day-old carcase without locating it and when they strayed too far the tigress called them back, until at last the buzzing flies helped them to find their meal.

As they get older, the cubs accompany the tigress on her hunting trips and by seven months they can kill for themselves – by then they will have grown to nearly six feet in length – but they can stay with their mother until they are two years old.

Young cubs will sometimes be undisciplined, playing with each other rather than concentrating on the hunt, and giving the alarm to the monkeys, fowl and hares that they begin by stalking. When they become more reliable, the tigress will lead them in stalking prey. She will make the first attack, holding down the prey while the cubs come in to learn to make the kill by biting the throat or the nape of the neck. As they copy their mother's example they gradually learn to become independent.

67

A tiger's territory

There have been instances of tigresses with cubs of different ages, but in these cases there has probably been only one surviving cub from the earlier litter and remating has taken place earlier than usual. In most cases the tigress will not mate until the cubs are ready to fend for themselves. Then she will call for a mate when she is in season and leave her scent to advertise her need. Courtship may last as little as two weeks, but during this period the male will not let another near, and will fight for possession of the female. She will be cautious at first but when tiger and tigress are sure that the other does not constitute a threat she may parade before him running her tail across his back. Meanwhile her cubs must go and find new territory for, although an adult male may be prepared to share his hunting ground with one or several females, he is unlikely to tolerate other younger males. A tiger's territory may range from twenty-five to several hundred square miles, and he will mark it by spraying urine and scent from glands at the base of the tail to let other tigers know that it is occupied. Tigers must range over wide areas looking for new or better territories, for when an established tiger dies or is shot its place is quickly taken by another.

For most of the cat family the pattern will be similar, although the duration of parental care will vary. Cougars, for instance, stay with their mothers for about two years and lynxes through the winter to the spring when they are about one year old.

Top At the beginning of courtship, a lioness may be very aggressive. **Above** There are at least twenty lions in this pride in the Ngorongoro Crater in Tanzania

Top Lynxes stay with their mother right through the winter. **Above left** Lions display considerable affection for each other. **Above right** The cat family use their sensitive ears to locate movement, like this watchful Spanish lynx

Life in the pride

Lions may live in groups of up to thirty, so that their lives are conducted much more publicly than those of other cats. When a female comes on heat she will attract males from some distance around and a fight may ensue. When the lioness is a member of a pride she will usually go off with its leader. Although they may make friendly gestures, such as rubbing up against each other, any sexual advance on the male's part is at first rejected. If he dares to put a paw upon her haunches she will probably reply with angry spitting and a clout. But this is not a serious quarrel – by their facial expressions and many little gestures both know that this is a formality. If the lioness walks off, the lion doggedly follows. After several hours, or even days, of persistent courtship he is accepted.

Lions will affectionately lick their mates and in their excitement give them plenty of nips and scratches. Coupling takes only a matter of seconds and is frequently completed by the male biting the lioness on the forehead. Over a period of four days, mating will probably take place six or eight times a day.

This is a dangerous time for the boss lion of the pride, for it is now that the other lions in the pride may make a bid to take over the leadership. The rival will creep up on the couple and force a fight. At first this will just be a vocal battle, but if roars and growls and snarls do not establish dominance it will come to blows. According to the observations of Norman Carr, when game warden of Kafue National Park, the lion keeps its claws retracted when fighting with a member of its own pride and relies on the force of its blows. These alone would break a human neck, but lions are protected by their shaggy manes, which act as shock absorbers.

If the boss lion maintains his dominance, the rival will return to the pride and the pattern will continue as before, a similar sequence following with the next female in the pride to come in season. When their 'honeymoon' is over, lion and lioness will rejoin their colleagues. The dominant animal apparently bears no resentment against the rebel—but if the rival triumphs he then must win over the rest of the pride. If the pride is a big one he may not succeed, and the pride will split into two groups. In a small pride, defeat will probably mean that the deposed lion must go in search of a new territory. Where lion territories border directly on each other, as they do over large parts of East Africa, he is unlikely to oust an existing occupant, so may be forced to live in arid areas where food is scarce and, as he becomes older and weaker, increasingly difficult for him to catch.

Where lions prey on migratory herds, as for instance in the Serengeti plain, they will not lay claim to a particular territory, and elsewhere they will sometimes tolerate an overlap if there is sufficient game.

The lion's cubs

When the lioness senses that she is nearing the time to give birth, she leaves the pride, often taking as a companion another female, either one too old to have cubs or a fully grown female from her last litter. The Masai call this companion 'Auntie' and it is her job to help with the confinement and in providing food and protection for the mother and her new-born cubs. The litter will be born in some sheltered spot where the cubs are safe from enemies if left alone, but where water is near and game not too far distant. The lion cubs will be born blind and open their eyes at about the sixth day. They have a spotted coat, and several black rings at the end of the tail, which lacks the final tuft of the adult lion.

When the lioness has recovered her strength she may go back to hunting with the pride, but she will leave the cubs carefully hidden in thick bushes or rock clefts and she and 'auntie' will viciously defend them from any apparent threat. They are weaned when they are about two-and-a-half months and given meat which is brought back to the den in the mouth and regurgitated for them. When they can manage to digest it, the kill may be dragged back for them to eat their share.

Opposite page Lions take a fatherly interest in their cubs. **Top right** Thomson's gazelle is typical of the smaller prey which a lioness will teach her cubs to kill. **Center right** The lioness will carry her cubs to a safe hiding place **Bottom right** Lion cubs are weaned at about two and a half months. **Above** At the end of mating, the lion will often bite the lioness's head

Norman Carr observed that when cubs were about three months old they were ceremonially led from the den and introduced to the other members of the pride. This ensured that they were known to the other lions and would not be attacked or killed as intruding strangers. Lions can display great affection once they have recognized a friend, running forward and nuzzling each other, but with an unknown lion the reception can be savage. The restraint shown when fighting for leadership with another member of the pride is forgotten and sometimes the whole pride will attack and kill an intruder.

The cubs' father will show an interest in his children and considerable tolerance towards them, but, unless the lion population has fallen particularly low and needs replenishment, the cubs eat last, which leads to dietary deficiencies, particularly of vitamins, and this partly accounts for the high death rate among cubs. Their mother teaches them how to skin prey with their claws and how to squeeze out the contents of the intestines by sliding them through their teeth, and gives them their first lessons in catching prey by encouraging them to stalk the tassel on the end of her tail. The cubs will practise on almost anything that moves, a butterfly, a dry leaf and particularly their brothers and sisters.

The cubs will stay with their mother until they are able to hunt for themselves, and then males may be driven from the pride if the leading lion fears their rivalry. Like a deposed leader of a pride, young lions must then find a territory where they will be tolerated. Often young males from local prides will band together, but at this age they lack hunting experience and are vulnerable to both injury and starvation.

Hunting techniques

With the exception of the cheetah, which can outrun its prey, the cat family all rely upon stealth to gain their food. Although they can make powerful leaps and reach high speeds over short distances—a lion may reach forty miles per hour for a very short burst—they have to get within close range of prey without being detected if they are to be successful. Their methods are clearly illustrated by a domestic cat stalking a piece of paper: the flattened body to make it less conspicuous, the soundless step, the instant stillness, the circuitous approach using all available cover, all these are typical. It has been suggested that many kills are made by the big cats lying in wait for prey by salt licks and waterholes, but animals know they are vulnerable at these places and take special care, so they would be more likely to scent the predator. The tree-climbing cats will lie in wait on a branch ready to drop on prey as it passes beneath and others may lie up in cover for hours watching a track they know is used by game. Their motionless patience is one of their greatest assets.

Ocelots, who are particularly skilled at catching birds, never lie in ambush but make a direct attack on all their prey.

Most of the cat family are nocturnal hunters and they are equipped with particularly good sight. The pupils of their eyes can contract to the narrowest slit (in *felis*) or the smallest circle (in *panthera*) to protect the eye from damage when the light is very bright, and open to a full circle which will admit all available light when it is dark. Focus and pupil control are very rapid so that, for instance, they can adjust as an animal they are watching moves from bright sunshine into shadow. To increase their sensitivity at night, they have a reflecting layer behind the retina known as the *tapetum lucidum*. Light which has not been absorbed in its passage through the cells of the retina is reflected back through them by this layer, thus doubling the strength of the information received. It is this light, reflected back out of the eye, that gives the eyeshine which can make a cat's eyes look like two points of fire in the night.

Left Lions can reach 40 mph for short bursts
Opposite page The lions of the Lake Manyara district of Tanzania are good climbers, happily sunning themselves in the trees, and in Kenya, **bottom left**, a lioness was photographed as she relaxed in a Euphorbia tree

A bobcat's mottled coat, **right,** helps to conceal it from both prey and enemy and, like most of the cat family, **below** it makes maximum use of cover when hunting. This bobcat's catch, **bottom,** is comparatively small, but larger cats angle for much bigger fish. Jaguars have been seen fishing for the 400-pound priarucu

With this sensitive sight, and the soundless step given by their padded paws and infinitely careful tread, the big cats can roam through the jungle or along ravines and tracks at night, alert for the sound of game but hidden by darkness and spared the watchful eyes of the sleeping monkeys and other sentries who in daytime would scream their warnings to the rest of the world.

When big cats twitch their tails while stalking, this is probably deliberate and distracts the prey's attention from the movement of the body. South American Indians consider that the jaguar lures his prey by the hypnotic swishing of his tail. They also believe that the jaguar can imitate the call of many animals and birds to attract them to it, and certainly tigers can make a call like that of sambar deer. In Sumatra they have been reported deliberately to mimic the calls of the wapiti deer and the buffalo.

Fishing cats

In Vietnam, a small race of tigers living in marshy land is reputed quietly to approach the waterside and sit with the tip of the tail dangling in the water, angling for fish. If one bites it is

Whether in a tree or on the ground, the leopard's spots make it difficult to see. Its camouflage is so effective that it was copied by the US forces for their jungle troops in World War 2. **Top right** A leopard lodges a reedbuck in a treefork, out of reach of thieves

instantly flicked out of the water on to the bank. There are more reliable records of ocelots and lynxes fishing and fish may form a considerable part of the jaguar's diet. Often they will simply scoop fish out of the water – not quite so difficult as it sounds when you consider that there are fish in the Amazon more than nine feet in length – but jaguars also tap the surface of the water with their tails to imitate the falling of fruit pods and berries on the water and attract the various species of fish which eat them. Amerindian tradition also says that jaguars will deliberately dribble saliva on to the water to attract fish, which are then scooped up but are not eaten until a worthwhile number has been collected. This behavior seems similar to that which a French hunter called Defosse observed when watching a leopard in Indo-China catching frogs. Having stunned one with its paw, it bit the head off and then placed it on a pile on the bank, continuing until it had collected a reasonable number to eat.

A leopard by lake Kariba, wild cats on the coast of Scotland and lions have all been seen catching fish. Despite popular belief to the contrary, most of the big cats are reasonable swimmers and some take a real pleasure in water.

Group strategy

Like other cats, lions will hunt alone but members of a pride often co-operate in a communal hunting strategy. The pride will split into several groups, apparently co-ordinated and kept in touch by tail flicking and other visual signals. One party will position itself upwind of the prey, perhaps a herd of impala or wildebeest, another will station itself on the flank and the greatest number will lie in ambush downwind. The first group rush the herd which takes flight, is deflected by the group on the flank and flees straight into the waiting ambush. A whole pride of lions will lie motionless in hiding for an hour or more waiting for the moment to carry out an attack. (Pairs of lions will carry out similar strategy, one going upwind and flushing out the prey whilst the other waits in ambush poised for the attack.) It is usually the lionesses of a pride which make the kill but it is the lions, and the boss lion first, who have first pickings of the meat (hence our expression 'the lion's share'), next the females, then the adolescents and the cubs.

The cheetah

While the other cats must stalk their prey undetected until they are close enough to make a last desperate dash, the cheetah's prodigious speed enables it to attack from a much greater distance. It will slowly approach a herd of antelopes or gazelles from downwind, freezing instantaneously if it suspects that one of them is looking in its direction. When within convenient range it will sprint forward and be on its quarry before the beast has had time to realize it is in danger. Gazelle and antelope are themselves fleet-footed animals, and the cheetah does not always succeed. If the quarry gets a good start the cheetah will drop out, exhausted by its burst of speed. The inflexible foot formation which enables the cheetah to move so fast also prevents it from swerving off its course, and since it cannot stop quickly at its high speed these factors alone may lose it a kill.

Cheetahs often hunt in pairs. Their young soon learn to keep a watchful eye for game, and, **below**, already have the fluid movements of their mother

A kill in Kruger National Park. **Left to right and top to bottom**
A lioness rushes out of cover at the approach of two impala to a
drinking place on the Sabi River. As she brakes for the final spring one
impala leaps over her and escapes but the lioness prepares herself for
the second animal and strikes it down, sinking her teeth into the
impala's neck to make the kill. When the ram is down, the other
members of the pride come in to share the meal

The kill

With small prey and with the smaller cats, the kill will often be made as a domestic cat catches
a mouse, ending a final rush with a pounce in which the hindfeet are kept firm on the ground to
give stability while the forepaws grasp the prey. With larger animals, the means of killing
must depend on the circumstances and the type of prey. Exact observation is extremely
difficult. A typical method would to be spring upon the animal's back, dragging it down by
sheer weight and breaking the neck by seizing the muzzle and pulling it sharply back, or the
throat may be bitten or the neck broken by a blow of the paw. There have even been cases of
taking the whole head in the mouth to produce asphyxiation. An inexperienced big cat may have
great difficulty in killing an animal outright and young lions have been seen eating an animal
that was not yet dead. Leopards, on the other hand, almost always make a clean kill, sinking
their teeth into the throat.

Once dead, the animal will usually be dragged away to cover, preferably to somewhere
near water, for after his exertions the victor is thirsty and exhausted. Having eaten well and
drunk sufficiently, he will take a long nap somewhere safe, returning to the kill for a second
gorging later, if nothing occurs to scare him off and it is not discovered by other carnivores
while he is away. A leopard may lodge his kill high up in the fork of a tree, out of the reach
of others, where for some unknown reason, vultures seem to respect the ownership of the body,
and do not touch it.

Old age

Sickness and injury, the blunting of the teeth by use and the loss of speed and strength that come with age mean that the carnivore has an even more difficult task in killing the prey that he must eat if he is to survive. He will be forced to give up the attempt to strike down the larger animals and concentrate on catching small ones that he would previously had disdained. If there is a challenge for his territory from a younger beast, he will probably be forced into country where prey is hard to find. Even the lion, long ago cast out from his pride, becomes a bag of bones. Eventually he too may become a meal for hyenas or for hunting dogs, a sad and sorry end for a once majestic beast.

Above After mother has had first taste, the cheetah cubs are called in to share a Grant's gazelle. **Left** Hunting is thirsty work; drinking are cougars **top**, lions, **middle**, and cheetah

The tyger

Tyger! Tyger! burning bright
In the forests of the night,
What immortal hand or eye
Could frame thy fearful symmetry?

In what distant deeps or skies
Burnt the fire of thine eyes?
On what wings dare he aspire?
What the hand dare seize the fire?

And what shoulder, and what art,
Could twist the sinews of thy heart?
And when thy heart began to beat,
What dread hand? and what dread feet?

What the hammer? what the chain?
In what furnace was the brain?
What the anvil? what dread grasp
Dare its deadly terrors clasp?

When the stars threw down their spears,
And water'd heaven with their tears,
Did he smile his work to see?
Did he who made the Lamb make thee?

Tyger! Tyger! burning bright
In the forests of the night,
What immortal hand or eye,
Dare frame thy fearful symmetry?

William Blake (1757–1827)

Out of the wild

The modern zoological garden is a comparatively recent development dating from the end of the eighteenth century, but the keeping of exotic animals goes back to very ancient times. The challenge to train or domesticate wild and savage animals seems also to be one which was taken up long ago.

One of the treasures found in the tomb of Tutankhamun is a gold shrine on a panel on which the young pharaoh is shown shooting wildfowl with his tame lion by his side; it was probably trained as a retriever. Queen Hatshepsut of Egypt is known to have had a menagerie which included leopards, and the pharaoh Rameses II was accompanied into battle by his lion Antamnekht, which went in front of his chariot alongside the horses and with a blow of his paw struck down anyone who dared come near.

As well as hunting with their trained or domesticated lions, the pharaohs also went out in their chariots to hunt the wild lion as the royal game.

In Assyria, where big cats were also trained, lions appear to have been captured and then released at a more convenient place for the royal sport. A magnificent set of sculptured bas-reliefs from Nineveh (now in the British Museum) depict all stages of a lion hunt, from the king making a ritual offering before the hunt to the party returning home carrying the bodies of the slain animals. One section shows lions being released from a cage. Another shows servants carrying nets, presumably to catch those animals which survived for another occasion.

The Persians kept large numbers of wild animals, including lions and other big cats, in great game parks and used to stage spectacular combats in which lions were matched against bulls. Alexander the Great took up this barbarous kind of entertainment and set lions to fight against dogs, and even against men, although he also kept tame lions as pets.

Above A carved relief from the palace of Ashurbanipal shows lions being released from their cages for the royal hunt, the king fighting on foot, and the king pouring a libation over dead lions. **Left** Lion and nobles in one of the Assyrian 'paradise parks'. **Opposite page** A lion from the Lake Manyara district

Thrown to the lions

The Romans began to keep wild animal collections during the third century BC but it was not until 185 BC that Marcus Fulvius Nobilior, returning from a campaign in Greece, introduced the hunting and killing of lions as a spectacle in the Roman amphitheaters. For the next forty years, public butchery was still only an occasional entertainment but from 146 BC such shows became more frequent throughout Italy. The prætor Lucius Sulla, having received a present of lions from Bochus, king of Mauretania, provided 100 male lions to be killed in the arena. Pompey gave a show in the Circus Maximus which included 600 lions and lionesses, as well as twenty elephants and the first rhinoceros ever seen in Rome. Julius Cæsar presented 400 lions, and the first giraffe. In his menagerie, the emperor Augustus had 260 lions and 420 'tigers' (which were probably cheetahs), and Nero had 300 lions and a pet tigress called Phœbe, which sat beside him at table and was occasionally allowed to make a meal of a human victim. After the opening of the Colosseum in 80 AD, when 5000 animals died in the inaugural show, the demand for wild beasts was enormous. At one time there were 11,000 wild animals held in the imperial forest reserves south of Rome. Hunting of lions to send to Italy is thought to have played an important part in the disappearance of the lion from North Africa.

Not all the lions in Rome were there for the arena, although perhaps when they got old, or if they turned bad tempered, that is where they might end up. As well as Nero's pet we know that Caracalla had a favorite lion called Acinaces, which used to join him at mealtimes and in his bedchamber, and Caligula, Nero's uncle, supplemented his pet lion's diet of goat with an occasional felon. Heliogabalus used to play frightening tricks upon his friends with lions and other beasts whose claws and teeth had been extracted, and he also used to enjoy driving a chariot drawn by four lions or tigers. These animals were no doubt carefully looked after as valuable possessions. Their manes were often powdered with gold dust and their necks decked with jewels. To be the master of the strong and beautiful King of Beasts must have seemed a fitting role to emperors who also saw themselves as gods.

Trained animals and circus acts also delighted the Romans and a surprising incident recorded at one amphitheater performance, in which hares being chased by hounds escaped by jumping into the open mouths of gentle lions, sounds like a particularly fine piece of animal training.

Opposite page A fanciful reconstruction of lions and tigers being released into the

Colosseum **Above** The Prince of Wales (later King Edward VII) tiger-shooting in India in 1876

Royal menageries

After the disintegration of the Roman empire, we have no knowledge of menageries or tamed wild animals being kept in Europe until in the eighth century Charlemagne, the king of the Franks who sought to unit all Christendom, took an interest in exotic species, and other rulers sent him presents of wild animals, including a lion which arrived as a gift from the Emir of Cairo.

At the beginning of the twelfth century, Henry I of England built up a big collection of animals including lions, leopards and lynxes, which he kept at his palace of Woodstock near Oxford. Two centuries later, Henry III moved the menagerie to the capital and installed his beasts in the Tower of London. Here were housed three splendid leopards sent as a present in 1235 by Frederick II, Holy Roman Emperor, in token of the three leopards of England which appeared on Henry's coat of arms. That year Frederick married Henry's sister Isabella and she found him an even greater enthusiast for wild animals than her brother. Their wedding procession included lions, panthers and cheetahs, and at their German court he ran a training school for cheetahs.

For a lion owned by Edward II, the sheriffs of London had to supply a quarter of a sheep and three sous a day, and for a leopard in the Tower sixpence for the leopard's food and three-halfpence for the keeper's diet. Under Edward III, the sums had increased to two shillings and one penny for meat for 'one lion, one leopard and two cat lions' and twelve sous for their attendants. Over the next century, the Tower lions died out and were not replaced, although the menagerie itself continued.

Meanwhile, on the Continent, Philip IV of France, known as Philip the Fair, had lions

83

Above Siberian tiger. **Opposite page** Lion cub
Left Bengal tiger; people have long been
fascinated by the sight of exotic animals but it is
only in the last century that we have learned to
care for them properly in captivity

Right London Zoo in 1849. The lion house is one of the older parts of London Zoo and new houses are planned for the big cats in the near future. A tiger, **below left**, black panther, **below right** (note the way this leopard's spots are still visible), and a lioness with cubs, **bottom**, in the old house

in his menagerie, and the exiled popes in Avignon set up a lion house. In the Netherlands, a fourteenth-century Count of Holland included lions in his menagerie at The Hague, and a nobleman in Ghent kept a lion tied near the entrance gate of his cattle to act as a watch-dog. (A later owner of the same castle kept four lions and made a deal with the local butcher to supply meat and an attendant for the lions in return for a set fee and the right to charge visitors for showing them. The butcher got the worst of the bargain, for no one seemed to be interested in seeing the lions.) In Amsterdam, there was a lion house which the city decided to keep stocked with a collection of lions as a symbol of independence after it achieved its municipal constitution in 1340.

Afonso V of Portugal, who conducted several wars in Africa, built up a menagerie of African animals in his castle at Cintra and he often sent lions as presents to friendly rulers. He may have contributed a lion – and certainly sent monkeys – to swell the collection of René of Anjou, which became famous throughout Europe. When René's daughter Margaret married the English king Henry VI, one of his courtiers gave her a lion as a wedding present, and the animal enclosures at the Tower were rebuilt and the collection enlarged. Here the

Right Two lion cubs placed in the Tower of London menagerie in 1823 were allowed to roam among the visitors for the first twelve months after their arrival. When grown, the lioness was inadvertently let out of her den and refused to return. An under-keeper 'had the boldness, alone and armed only with a stick, to venture upon the task of driving her back into her place of confinement; which he finally accomplished, not however without strong symptoms of resistance on her part, as she actually made three springs upon him. all of which he was fortunate enough to avoid.' Following the birth of cubs, this lioness refused the least familiarity on the part of her keepers
Below Detail from the *Journey of the Magi* by Benozzo Gozzoli (see overleaf)

queen (a tough monarch who led an army during the Wars of the Roses and earned Shakespeare's description of 'tiger's heart wrapped in a woman's hide') staged combats of lions against tigers to entertain her court. The animals' cages and their keepers' quarters were in and around the fortification known as the Lion Tower (now demolished) and later monarchs kept a menagerie there for another four centuries.

Another recipient of presents from Afonso V was the French king Louis XI, who also received animals from other princes, including a cheetah from the Duke of Ferrara which had been trained to chase hares. Louis also had a lion which slept at the foot of his bed. Francis I also kept a cheetah for hunting, which rode pillion on a cushion behind its keeper.

A painting of the three Magi on their way to Bethlehem which Piero de 'Medici commissioned for the chapel of the Medici Palace in Florence, shows members of his family and various allied princes as the three wise men and their entourage, and includes a portrait of the Duke of Lucca, whose emblem was a leopard, with a leopard riding pillion behind him in just this way.

Above A pride of lions in the Serengeti National Park of Tanzania, in the heart of the African lion's natural territory. **Left** Feeding time in Brisbane Lion Park. There are no native members of the cat family in Australia. **Opposite page** A tiger in captivity eats a meal provided by man

The Medici had a fine menagerie of their own. Piero's father, Cosimo, had a special arena built for a visit of Pope Pius and the Sforzas, in which he released ten lions and other wild beasts to fight for their entertainment. However, on this occasion the lions disappointed him and lay down and slept. Before the show they had been paraded through the streets with the boars, wolves, bulls and other animals, so perhaps they were tired, or just well fed already. Lorenzo de' Medici–'the Magnificent', Cosimo's other son–built up the Florence menagerie until it became the pride of the city. Here the great painters of the renaissance could see living specimens from which to paint the animals in their pictures. Another Medici, Pope Leo X, established a menagerie at the Vatican, which included lions and leopards, and many other Italian noblemen established rival animal collections.

The increasing interest in exotic animals and their use was stimulated by the growing contacts with Africa and the East, whether through wars, Crusades, trade or exploration. In Africa, the Middle East and Asia, Arab princes and eastern emperors had continued to use cheetahs as hunting dogs as the Egyptians and Assyrians had done in antiquity.

Oriental hunters

When Marco Polo traveled in China in the thirteenth century, he found that Kublai Khan kept great animal parks and employed 'a great number of leopards, lynxes and lions in his hunting. When he rides on horseback through his parks of animals he frequently takes with him several leopards which are mounted pillion behind their keepers. Thus they are ready, when given the word of command, to give chase to a deer or antelope.' Perhaps Polo's knowledge of big cats was deficient and the lions were in fact tigers or one of the smaller big cats, for he describes the lions used for hunting as having 'a thick, glossy coat marked with bands of black, white and red.'

In India, nearly three centuries later, the Mogul emperor Akbar hunted with trained cheetahs. Pictures painted about 1590 show cheetahs being captured in traps, and hunting scenes that enable us to understand how these cats were used. The cheetahs were taken to the hunting ground on litters, their eyes covered with a hood like a falcon's. They were then transferred to a seat on horseback behind their keeper–or perhaps some actually traveled in that position. Then they would be sent after the quarry like coursing hounds. They would strike the victim down with a blow of the paw and wait for their master to complete the kill.

In our own century, the Maharajah of Kolhapur kept a large stable of hunting cheetahs. He imported the animals from Kenya and trained them to chase black buck. They were taught to kill only males, which have darker coats than females, and to encourage this, food was brought to them only by men wearing dark clothes, while their regular attendants (two to each cat) wore light-colored garments. The cheetahs lived in a large dormitory, each with its own platform-like bed, and except when actually hunting, being fed or being exercised, they were kept hooded by a black mask tied over the eyes.

When a hunt was planned the cheetahs were taken by car or truck to a plain where there were plentiful herds of black buck and released to course after them for the amusement of the Maharajah and his friends. If they struck down a female they were punished by having the carcase taken from them but otherwise were allowed to eat some of their kill before it was removed to be used as venison.

The Maharajah also tried to train leopards but did not achieve any success with them.

Imperial lions

In Africa, in the kingdom of Ethiopia, it has long been the custom and the prerogative of the emperor to keep a collection of domesticated lions. The lion is both the symbol of the Crown and of the State, and Haile Selassie, the present ruler, keeps up the tradition. Lions roam around the palace apartments in Addis Abbaba and, in the tradition of monarchs of the past, he makes occasional presents of a lion to other rulers and friendly states.

The first zoological gardens

The popularity of the menageries in Europe fluctuated. At the Tower of London, the royal collection continued, with others at Windsor and at Kew. In 1657, during the Commonwealth, there were six lions; in 1708, eleven lions, two leopards and a tiger; but, although there were additions during the next half century, by 1822 there were no big cats at all–only 'the grizzly bear, an elephant and one or two birds.' In France, there was a resurgence of interest in private menageries when Louis XIV developed a passion for animals and built a small zoo in the gardens at Versailles. In Italy the great Florentine collection had been dispersed, and the

The cheetah is the fleetest animal on earth
Right The Mogul emperor Akbar hunting
Below Cheetah belonging to the Gaekwar of Baroda, who also kept hunting cheetahs

Above and opposite page Cheetahs and cubs

Portuguese royal collection was no more, but the Prince of Orange still had a menagerie at Loo in the Netherlands at the end of the eighteenth century, when the French swept in during the Revolutionary Wars.

Visitors had always been permitted at the Tower of London on payment of a small fee 'to see the lions'—and the collection there became a much better one after Alfred Cops became Keeper of the lions in 1822—but the first public zoological garden was in Paris. In 1793, the animals from the royal collection at Versailles and, later, the survivors of the Dutch menagerie, were taken to the Jardin des Plantes. There, for the first time, really scientific study could be made of living specimens.

The scientific value and general popularity of the Paris zoo encouraged the formation of the Zoological Society of London which opened the Zoological Gardens in Regent's Park in 1828. The Society soon gained royal patronage and in 1830 William IV presented all the animals from Windsor. A year later, he gave the animals from the Tower to be divided between London and a new zoo opening in Dublin (where the first lion cubs to be bred and reared in captivity were born twenty-one years later). Two other English zoos soon followed: Bristol and Belle View, Manchester, both opening in 1836.

Trophy hunters
While people at home began to flock to the zoological gardens, Europeans overseas sought to emulate the kings and princes of the past and display their virility by going out to kill wild animals in their natural habitat. Even in the days when men went out to hunt with spear and bow and arrow, they had made a difference to the survival of the lions of North Africa; with firearms, hunters began the extermination of several species. While it is possible to admire the courage of the true hunter, of the man or woman who goes out to eliminate a man-eater or a persistent thief of domestic livestock, the trophy collector who fires from the back of an elephant or from a truck, behind the safety of a barbed wire screen, is simply a killer himself.

Housing the big cats

As the zoos gained experience in caring for their animals, attitudes to their housing and presentation began to change. Instead of providing heated indoor houses, it was found that exercise and space were more important in keeping an animal happy and healthy, and that some species from even quite hot climates could happily adjust to northern winters. One of the first people to organize a zoo in this way was Carl Hagenbeck of Hamburg, who, with his father, became one of the world's largest animal dealers, the owner of a fine circus and the director of one of Europe's greatest zoos.

Hagenbeck, whose favorite animals were the big cats, wanted to present his animals so that visitors would see them as closely as possible to how they would appear in nature. Instead of cages with bars, he planned ditches and moats to prevent the animals escaping, and built artificial cliffs, caves and panoramas to suggest their native habitat. At his zoo at Stellingen, near Hamburg, he built an artificial 'glen' to house his carnivores with an inner den where they could retire for shelter or privacy. Here his lions and tigers happily exercised in all weathers, in sun and snow. Such was their ability to adapt that they grew thicker fur as a protection from the cold.

In his autobiography, Hagenbeck gives many instances of the friendly relationship he had with his animals, even when they had been long separated. One tiger which, as the result of a bad cold, developed an eye condition that made him nearly blind, was daily nursed by the zoo director and completely recovered. He and his mate were sold to the Berlin zoo, but to the end of the tiger's life he recognized Hagenbeck whenever he visited there. 'He would always fall into the most violent excitement on hearing my voice in the distance; and when I came up he would purr like a cat, and was never satisfied till I had gone into the cage and spent some little time with him.'

A lion family in a natural enclosure at Bronx Zoo, New York

94

On a visit to the Zoological Gardens in the Bronx, New York, two lions and a tiger who had spent some time in his care long before, became attentive as soon as he approached their den. They 'stared at me like a human being who saw a familiar face but could not put a name to it. But the moment I called out the names by which I used to address them in Hamburg they sprang up and ran to the bars, purring loudly when I stroked and caressed them.'

Hagenbeck certainly seems to have inspired confidence in his animals. One old lion which he had had either in circus or zoo for eighteen years so trusted him that, although in pain, he calmly lay down as he was ordered and allowed two pairs of claws, which had grown too long and entered the flesh on his hind feet, to be cut and extracted. Indeed, Hagenbeck believed that all carnivores, if caught young and treated properly, were capable of being brought up as domestic pets. With a good-tempered animal and a patient owner that is no doubt true, but it is not a theory for anyone to put into practice unless they have a zoo or a palace park to keep them in! He goes on to say: 'Their so-called wild nature does not break out unless something happens to put the animals in a rage; and this, after all, is just the same with domestic animals.' However, he omits to add, a tiger's weight, teeth and claws, should he be 'put into a rage', can do more serious harm than those of a domestic cat.

Top Cougar (Puma, or Mountain Lion). Wild lions, **above**, gain vitamins from the stomach contents of their prey. Lions in captivity, **left**, have to be given vitamin supplements
Opposite Joan Embery, Miss Zoofari of San Diego Zoo, walks Toby to a personal appearance

Training animals

Another of Hagenbeck's preoccupations was the training of wild animals. He was horrified by the cruel whips and red-hot irons which were so often employed, and he believed that a gentle training based on trust and kindness would be equally effective. He established a circus in 1887, and employed a trainer who would follow his methods. He began his experiments with dogs and then went on to lions. He began with twenty-one cats but decided that only four seemed to have any aptitude. His training was based on a system of rewards and punishments.

Mary Chipperfield, a present-day British animal trainer who develops a very close relationship with her animals, raising many of them by bottle in her own home, believes that the easiest big cats to train for performance are those which are less gentle and domesticated. Some will do tricks because they enjoy them and they want to please their trainer. Sometimes they will invent a trick for themselves, such as her tiger Sukie, who was encouraged to turn a playful roll on the ground into a controlled roll around the ring, but for most tricks she uses the animals' natural aggression in the training, egging the lions and tigers to 'come on' at her. If, for instance, she wants them to step from one rostrum to another she first places one between her and the cat and then encourages it to advance, and as the next stage adds a further rostrum which the animals must climb upon to reach her. To get an animal to jump from one stand to another she teaches them first to walk across two, then gradually begins to separate them until the walk becomes a jump and then a leap. All the time she has sufficient command over the animals to provoke their advance without permitting them to attack her.

With her lion Marquis, she achieved a very difficult feat, training him to ride on the back of her Spanish stallion Jarro. First she started taking the lion with her when she went to groom Jarro in his stable; then she left the lion chained in the stable for long periods, close enough for the two animals to get used to each other without actually being able to touch. She trained the horse to accept dogs jumping on to its back, gradually increasing the size of the dog, while Marquis was trained to climb on to circus pedestals and to jump from one to another. When the lion was used to a pedestal the height of the horse Jarro was put in its place one day and – Marquis became a jockey. It took four months to reach this point.

Mary Chipperfield thinks animals in captivity benefit from training since it gives them exercise and directed play that fills some of the gap left when they do not have to hunt for prey and do not have the freedom to invent their own group games with other animals.

Top Mary Chipperfield swimming with her favorite tiger, Sukie. **Above** A family of lion cubs at Longleat. **Left** A tired lion in the Lion Park, near Sydney, Australia

Lions in the National Parks of Kenya

Lion safari

Mary's father, Jimmy Chipperfield, was responsible for one of the biggest break-throughs ever in the presentation of big cats to the general public. In the game reserves of Africa, where animals are protected from wanton slaughter, tourists can travel in buses and cars and, if they are in the right place at the right time, observe lions in their natural state. Why not, he thought, a lion reserve in England? Already there were zoos such as Whipsnade, Bedfordshire, in the English countryside, where animals had space and privacy, which had proved that big cats could adapt to northern climates and, without the strain of living in a cage under the inescapable public gaze, could breed much more successfully. If the enclosure were carefully planned to ensure both the comfort of the lions and the safety of the visitors, it would be possible to keep lions in a more natural way so that visitors could observe their behavior at close hand, for if they stayed within their cars with the windows closed they would be quite safe from any accident.

Mr Chipperfield found an ally for his plan in the Marquis of Bath, owner of the magnificent Elizabethan mansion, Longleat House, Wiltshire. In the extensive park around this stately home they planned a wildlife safari. The scheme met considerable opposition, but once established became such a success that the Chipperfield family have organized ten other similar safari parks in England, Scotland, Canada, Holland and the USA, and elsewhere others have copied them.

At Tama Zoological Park in Japan they had a similar idea which, unknown to Jimmy Chipperfield, they were developing at about the same time, and which opened to the public a year before Longleat was ready. The system at Tama is a different one, in that the enclosure is an artificial area within an already existing zoo, and visitors are driven around in a specially armored bus, so that they lose a little of the proximity to the animals that is apparent when driving their own cars in the Chipperfield parks.

Caring for carnivores

Even the comparative freedom of a safari park is nevertheless a large cage, and although lions in these circumstances revert to much more natural behavior than when confined in a zoo, they still lead a life which is controlled by humans and very different from that in the wild. In this limited freedom, lions have the opportunity to form their own prides and to choose their mates, so that breeding is much more natural, but they are animals reared from birth with food provided and medical attention always on hand. Being well fed they have no need to hunt and, since lions are naturally lazy beasts, they pay little attention to the native animals that share their territory.

Lions in captivity raise more of their litters to maturity than in the wild, but there are still those in whom their mothers have no interest which must be raised by hand. One method is to find the cubs a foster mother for the first few weeks. At London Zoo they have often used a boxer or a collie dog, but if there is not a bitch in whelp available which is placid enough to accept a boisterous cub or cubs suckling on her every couple of hours for six to seven weeks, they must be fed by bottle.

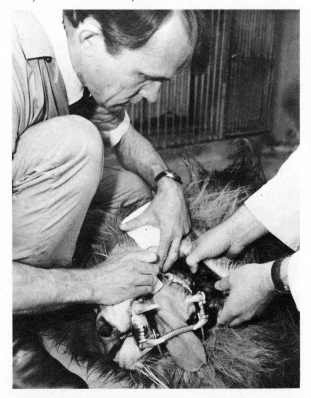

Above and left Caesar, an African lion, is given an anæsthetic and has his mouth wedged open before veterinarians can give treatment for his teeth. **Opposite page** Captive lions eat about 12 pounds of meat per day

A bottle-fed cub needs as much attention as a human baby. A human must do everything for it that its mother would: feed every two hours, wash, help with evacuation, clean up afterwards and provide a comforting and reassuring presence. Even when nearly adult, the lions Elsa, reared by Joy Adamson, and Marquis, reared by Mary Chipperfield, came to their foster mothers and demanded a thumb to suck for reassurance. They will go from the bottle to lapping up their milk, and slowly be transferred to solid food. At first a little minced meat will be mixed with the milk to be lapped up with it. Then they have a rib bone with the stringy bits removed as a joint to themselves and eventually go on to eat the normal adult ration. In a zoo where the cats are caged and do not have a great deal of exercise adult lions and tigers usually receive about twelve pounds of meat a day, six days a week, and leopards, jaguars, pumas and the smaller cats about six pounds or less. The Chipperfields also make one fast day each week.

For cubs raised by their mothers the pattern will be similar, for the mother will regurgitate meat when they are ready to be weaned to prepare them for solid food.

There is no real need to feed big cats with such regularity. In the wild they would gorge themselves on a kill and then not hunt again until they were hungry, but the public like to see a lively lion and since after eating a forty or fifty pound meal the animal would spend the next few days largely sleeping it off, the recipe is less, more often.

The meat which most carnivores are fed in captivity does not contain the amount of vitamins which wild animals obtain from the stomach contents and offal of their prey, and a vitamin supplement is therefore added to their water, or dusted on to their food, or occasionally given in tablets which are inserted into the meat. You cannot blow a pill down a lion's throat as you can with a horse's, or make it swallow one as you can a domestic cat, so drugs must be administered either by pushing pills into the meat – in which case it is difficult to make sure that the cat eats them – or by injection.

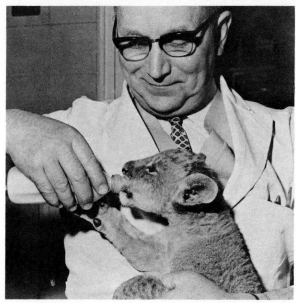

Opposite page and above The natural diet of a wild animal, like these lions in Kenya, has to be matched for that of a captive animal
Right Bottle-feeding at London Zoo

At one time, if a big cat needed medical attention it would have to be driven into a small closed crate and anæsthetized with chloroform, but today it can be put into a small close-barred cage and given an injected anæsthetic before being treated or taken to hospital. Where animals are ranging free, medication or anæsthetic can be given by means of darts which are fired into the muscle tissue without causing the animal pain.

Where animals have developed very close relationships with humans they may sometimes be treated without the need for any precautionary anæsthetic. Sometimes their relationship with humans can have a negative effect. Gussie, a London lion picked up when five days old in a Kenya game park and hand-reared, associates more closely with humans than with her own kind, and when she is in season she will have nothing to do with a lion and gives all her attention to her keeper.

Big cats are each individuals with their own tastes and preferences and it is not surprising that even when in season they will not take any male that is proferred, but captivity does seem to make some cats refuse males completely. With these exceptions lions are generally considered comparatively easy to breed, and so are pumas, but tigers are much more difficult and their cubs most often have to be hand-reared.

Musical lions

December 31, 1764

I thought it would be worthwhile to make an odd experiment. Remembering how surprisingly fond of music the lion at Edinburgh was, I determined to try whether this was the case with all animals of the same kind. I accordingly went to the Tower with one who plays on the German flute. He began playing near four or five lions; only one of these (the rest not seeming to regard it at all) rose up, came to the front of his den, and seemed to be all attention. Meantime, a tiger in the den started up, leaped over the lion's back, turned and ran under his belly, leaped over him again, and so to and fro incessantly. Can we account for this by any principle of mechanism? Can we account for it at all?

John Wesley in his Journal

Lions can be very aggressive but show great affection to their families

Mohammed finds the sharpest eyes

An Arab legend

One day the Prophet Mohammed decided to test the sight of all living creatures. He discovered that Allah had bestowed the gift of the best sight upon the horse and the lion, but the tests he had devised could not distinguish between them. It was clear that they could both see by night as readily as human beings can see by day, so he planned a test which would tax the sharpest eyes.

On the blackest night that ever was, he called the lion and the horse before him and placed in front of them two bowls. In one he poured some milk and floating upon it placed a single white hair. In the other there was pitch with a hair that was jet black. The horse was first to make a trial of his sight and he took out the white hair from the bowl of milk. Then the lion's turn came. He saw the black hair lying on the pitch and took that to the Prophet who decided that that was the harder test and announced that the lion had the sharpest eyes of any of Allah's creatures.

Above and top left White tigers at Bristol Zoo
Left One of the white tigers in Delhi Zoo

White Tigers

One spectacular breeding success of recent years has been a strain of white tiger. These are not a separate species but simply a color variation and they have been reported from several parts of the tiger's range, including Assam, India and north China.

They usually have all the normal tiger markings and characteristics, except that the ground color is white and the stripes dark brown or reddish black (so that they are also sometimes called 'red' tigers). True albinos can also occur but they are very rare. There were frequent reports of white tigers in the Indian state of Rewa, and in 1947 the Maharajah of Rewa had the idea of trying to capture one and breed a white strain in captivity. He believed that the white pigmentation was due to a recessive gene and that where two animals with the gene were mated half the offspring should be white. For four years a watch was kept on the jungles until, in 1951, a tigress was seen with a litter of four cubs, three of them with normal coloring and one, which was larger then the others, white. The mother and three cubs were shot and the white cub, a male, captured. He was given the name Mohan and reared at the Maharajah's palace, where the old harem was converted into dens ready for the experiment.

Tigers with the usual coloration

The following year, a well-grown tigress of normal coloring was captured and introduced to Mohan's den. In 1953, they bred and produced their first litter, of which all the cubs had normal coloring, as did litters born in 1955 and 1956. A female from the second litter was mated with Mohan when she reached maturity and in 1958 produced four cubs, *all* of which were white and three of them female. In 1960, Mohan and the same female produced a litter of two white males and a normal female, and in 1962, one white male and one white female. One of the females born in 1958 was sold to the Washington, DC, zoo in 1960, after which the Indian government banned further exports.

By 1963, the Maharajah had decided that he had achieved his aim and could no longer afford to continue his breeding program. He asked the government to allow him to sell one pair of the cubs and to accept the rest of the stock. After negotiations it was agreed that the pair born in 1962 could be exported and they were sold to Bristol Zoo in England for a figure of around £8000. The other tigers went to Indian zoos, two white males going to Calcutta, and Mohan and two females to Delhi, where further breeding has taken place. Meanwhile the Bristol pair settled happily in their new home and have bred successfully.

On safari

The men and women who protect the interests of wildlife may still have to cull animals who upset the ecological balance, or liquidate a man-eater, and since their charges can be very dangerous if they think that they or their young are threatened they may also carry arms to defend themselves – but for most people today a safari is to *see* the game and 'shoot' it with a camera, not to score up notches on a rifle butt.

The modern big game 'hunter' making safari in East Africa (and there were 125,000 visitors to Tanzanian national parks alone in 1971) flies in from Europe or America and can stay in luxuriously-appointed hotels and lodges in the heart of the reserves. He travels through the homelands of the lion and leopard in a comfortable mini-bus or private automobile. Cocktails by a swimming pool may seem strange on a holiday studying wildlife, but it is all part of the show. If from your hotel terrace, or the safety of Kenya's exotic Treetops Lodge built high among gnarled cape chestnut trees, you can watch animals coming to a salt-lick or a waterhole throughout the night, there will be no lack of excitement – despite the creature comforts.

The money brought in by tourists can play an important part in the economy of the new nations of Africa and is the only argument likely to carry much weight with national governments when the preservation of big cats and other wildlife is set against the needs of their people. To expect people to give up killing wild animals that have been either a source of danger or of food, and to ask them to leave good arable land to the lion and the leopard when an expanding population and the exhaustion of much of Africa's soil mean that there may not be enough for human needs, is asking a great deal – especially when the demand usually comes from Americans and Europeans who have long since killed off most of their own indigenous wildlife.

A people such as the semi-nomadic Masai, who do not hunt wild game and have for a century or more shared their territory with wild animals, still need schools, hospitals and other services and roads to reach them, all of which change the established natural balance. Many animals follow a regular migratory pattern, the big cat predators going along with their prey, and this can easily be disrupted by even quite small development across their route.

In the game parks and reserves a serious problem of the same kind exists. The new hotels, the roads to reach them, the housing to accommodate the people who staff them, the regular transport to bring them to and fro and the upheaval of the construction work involved are a damaging impact on the 'unspoiled' territories. It takes a month for the grass to recover from

On game reserves, the visitor in his automobile
can get a close-up view of wildlife, but the
effect of his presence has not yet been assessed

the passage of a tourist mini-bus – and if three buses follow the same track it will probably become permanent and the ecology will be disrupted. When a circle of automobiles surround a pride of lions, or a queue of buses slowly pass them at the roadside, they cannot help but interrupt their movement, particularly if it is late in the afternoon when they would normally begin to hunt. It is exciting to speed along beside a cheetah to film him going in to make a kill – but this would-be animal-lover may well cause the distraction that loses the cheetah his meal. Wildlife experts are seriously concerned that continual interruption and disturbance may prevent predators from getting enough food.

Scientists are only now beginning to study these effects, but it is possible that in the future there will have to be greater control over visitors on safari and a limit placed upon their numbers.

Snarls or yawns? **Opposite page top left** Cheetah. **Top right** Lioness. **Bottom left** Cougar **Top left** Leopard. **Top right** Lion cub **Above** Serval. **Left** Cougar cubs

Return to the wild

There are enough lions in zoos to maintain the species in captivity, but what is to be done if a ranger comes across an orphaned cub? No one who loves animals could leave it, too young to do anything for itself, to await death in the wild. Yet the alternative, to rear it by hand, would condemn it to a life in captivity, for not only would its own kind reject it because of its human association but it would be unable to hunt and unequipped to defend itself. At least, that is what everyone believed until recent years produced evidence that this need not be the case.

The patience and skill which can be applied to taming and training wild animals can be used to teach them to be wild. It is difficult enough to make an animal learn to do tricks to please humans, but for a human to replace a lion's mother and teach it to be a lion is a much more challenging task. Nevertheless, the experiment has been tried – and has succeeded.

After Kenyan game wardens had been forced to shoot a lioness during a hunt for a man-eater, they found three lion cubs hidden in a rock crevice. They were raised by Senior Game Warden George Adamson and his wife Joy. When they were about six months old two of the cubs were sent to Rotterdam-Blijdorp zoo, but the weakest of the litter, whom they named Elsa, stayed with them. She lived with them sharing their home and their tents when they were on safari. She was surrounded by natural prey and often chased animals – even driving them towards members of her pride – but she did not kill her own meat. She had to be taught and encouraged to turn her games into earnest and make her own kill. She had to learn to face the wild on its own terms without running back to human beings for help when frightened or uncertain. Eventually she made the necessary adjustment and, despite her long association with humans, gained acceptance from other lions. But she did not forget her human friends, bringing her cubs to show them, and was able to maintain contact and understanding in both worlds.

Opposite page Virginia McKenna as Joy Adamson in a scene from the film *Born Free*

Above Wakeful lioness. **Below** Lazy lion

The Adamsons have told the story of Elsa and her cubs, and that of Pippa, a leopardess, in Mrs Adamson's own best-selling books. A little later, Norman Carr achieved a similar success with two male cubs whose raising closely followed natural growth, for they do not appear to have become so dependent emotionally on Mr Carr as Elsa did on Joy Adamson. They were given carcases rather than cut meat as soon as they were ready to digest it. Nevertheless, at one stage it was necessary to shoot two wild lions to provide these two with a territory, as Norman Carr described in *Return to the Wild*.

George Adamson has had a similar success with other lions, perhaps most surprisingly with a lion born in a West of England zoo, sold by the pet department of a fashionable department store and reared by two young Australians in a London flat above an antique shop in Kings Road, Chelsea. Anthony Bourke and John Rendell called their lion Christian and tell his full story in their book *A Lion Called Christian*. From swinging London to the open skies of East Africa is a change to which many humans might find it difficult to adjust, but the patience and care of George Adamson were able to turn a lion who regularly went shopping in the trendiest boutiques into a happily adjusted and independent resident in the East African bush.

Below Lioness at a kill. **Left and opposite page** Tree climbing lioness near Lake Lagarja, Serengeti

Opposite page, above Lion cubs were probably the first big-cat young to be successfully reared in captivity. **Opposite page bottom, right and below** The fleet-footed cheetah was trained as a retriever many centuries ago but was not successfully bred in captivity until 1960
Above The long legs of the serval suggest that it chases its prey in the same way as the cheetah

Opposite page, above Lioness and cub
Opposite page, below Cheetah and cubs
Right and below Puma and her cub. The
female cat is usually a devoted mother

King of beasts and lord of forests

Lions appear in the royal arms of England, Scotland, Norway, Denmark, Bavaria, Bohemia and in the blazons of many other princes, peoples and places. For centuries the titular King of Beasts has stood for strength, courage, power and justice, even in countries that have not known a lion in historic times. His image has been used as a trademark to suggest quality and reliability. Presumably the earlier peoples gave him his title for his apparent natural superiority. He is noble in appearance, powerful in muscle and without a rival among the animals.

Above, opposite page and below Modern knowledge of the lion's way of life has not deposed him from his role as King of Beasts **Left** In the middle ages it was thought that a lynx's urine could turn into a precious stone

Victory over a lion was one way in which the heroes of early legend proved themselves. Gilgamesh, King of Uruk, is the hero of an epic from Mesopotamia dating back to more than 1500 years before Homer. In his search for paradise he kills the lions which guard the passes of the mountain Mashu, between the peaks of which the sun rises and sets and which is the gateway to paradise.

The great Greek demi-god Heracles was eighteen when he slaughtered a ferocious lion which ravaged the herds on the slopes of mount Kithairon. When, after killing his wife and children in a fit of madness, he had to perform twelve labors to expunge the guilt, the first labor was to exterminate the Nemean Lion. This beast was impervious to arrows and spears, for his skin could not be pierced. Heracles only succeeded in his task by grappling with the lion, hand to claw, until he succeeded in throttling it. Thereafter the hero wore the lion's skin which made him invulnerable.

The stories of Samson, the Israelite strongman, who also slew a lion with his bare hands, and Daniel, who survived being cast into a lion's den, are the best-known of the several episodes involving big cats which are described in the Old Testament.

The early medieval bestiarists in their would-be scientific descriptions of beast and fowl credit the lion with some unlikely attributes. Those with curly manes, they considered, will be peaceful, those with straight hair fierce; they are afraid of creaking wheels and terrified of fire; and they disguise their spoor by rubbing it with their tail. Their manners are excellent for they never overeat—or, if they do, use their paws to pull out the excess from their mouths. They are compassionate for they spare those who prostrate themselves before them and allow prisoners to return to their own countries. When the lioness gives birth the cubs are dead and lie so for three days until their father comes and breathes upon their faces and brings them to life.

The royal arms of Great Britain. The lion is one of the 'supporters' and also appears 'rampant', in the second quarter, representing Scotland. The three lions which represent England are termed 'leopards' in heraldry; they are not actually spotted, this is just the heraldic name for a lion 'passant guardant'

Above Saint Jerome and his lion, engraved by Albrecht Dürer. **Left** A winged lion, symbol of St. Mark, patron of the Venetians, who placed it on their overseas fortresses like this one in Greece. **Opposite page** 17th-century engraving of Androcles and the lion by Wenceslaus Hollar

Of the panther (really the leopard) they declared that when he awakes from sleeping off a good meal he will belch loudly, thereby emitting a perfume which is so sweet that when other animals hear the noise they follow him to catch its savor.

The lynx was thought to have an even stranger quality, for it was said that after seven days its urine hardens into a precious stone. Therefore they cover it up with sand 'from a certain constitutional meanness, for fear that the piss should be useful as an ornament to the human race.'

But these are literary ideas, the conceit of men of learning in lands far from the big cats' domain. In their own countries the cat family are often closely involved in folklore and superstition as well as having the important religious role described in 'god of the mountain and jungle.' In the east, a tiger's whiskers have special properties: in Malaya a tiger's whisker pulverized into a portion of a tiger's flesh is thought to make an efficient and deadly poison, while in Indonesia they could be burned and the powdered ash mixed into a drink as a remedy for impotence. Tiger fat could be used to treat rheumatism, and as a love potion, and tiger

Above Illuminations in a 12th-century bestiary illustrate some beliefs about the lion: he eats monkeys as a medicine, he is compassionate to prisoners, and he is afraid of white cocks. **Top right** Cougar or mountain lion. **Right** Contrary to popular belief, many of the cat family are capable swimmers, like this tiger, keeping cool in a stream

Top Reconstruction of a sabre-tooth tiger, one of the earliest forms of big cat. **Left and above** A tiger's fangs were once powdered as a cure for dog bites, and its whiskers burned and the ash used to remedy impotence. If a tiger was killed, its whiskers were singed or plucked out to prevent its spirit from revenging itself on the killer

Above Lions in Nairobi National Park. **Left** Emperor Haile Selassie upholds the tradition of keeping lions at the Ethiopian court where they walk at liberty—to the consternation of some of his diplomatic visitors

milk would cure eye complaints–if it could be obtained! Elsewhere, tiger blood is thought to be able to ward off the spirits that cause smallpox and measles, powdered tiger bones are a cure for dog bites, and in many places it is believed that to eat the flesh of the lion or the leopard will give a man the courage and strength of the animal.

Sir Alfred Pease, an English big game hunter, was traveling in Algeria in 1892 when he saw what appeared to be a freshly killed lion being carried across the back of a donkey. He stopped the man who led the donkey and his two companions to ask where they had killed the lion, at which one of them said 'Not dead,' and tugged on a rope around the lion's neck–making the animal scramble off the donkey. It was an old lion but a fine specimen and in good condition, but it had been blinded to make it more easy to control. This was a sort of sacred lion which they took from place to place to exorcize the evil spirits which cause sickness and to keep away the plague. Its powers must have been thought effective, for it was in great demand and its keepers earned a good income for taking it into the houses of the sick.

The respect with which eastern peoples treat the tiger, the Lord of the Forest, prevents them from refering to the tiger by name lest he appear, and the Moi mountain people of Vietnam believe that the tiger hears everything that is said, so they are always very careful of what they say. In India, Malaya and China the ghost of the victim of a man-eating tiger is widely thought to sit on the tiger's head and point out as the next victim anyone who has betrayed the tiger's movements to a hunter. Contrarywise, some folk traditions say that the victim will warn the hunter of the tiger's approach, thereby achieving a sort of revenge.

In Sumatra, people believe that a tiger may be spiritually linked with a man, befriending him, and that people with no dip in their upper lips are 'ngelmo'–tiger men–who can change their shape into that of a tiger. The medicine-men of South America are also thought to be able to turn into jaguars, and in some tribes a hunter who kills a jaguar is believed to be taken over by the jaguar's spirit.

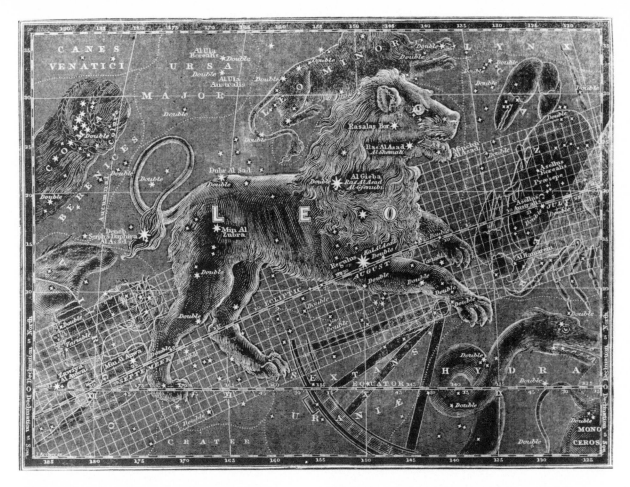

Above The constellation Leo which gives its name to the fifth sign of the zodiac. **Below** The English animal artist, George Stubbs (1724–1806), who painted numerous pictures of lions made this study of a trained cheetah which used to hunt in Windsor Great Park

In East Africa, some tribes believe that the souls of the dead chiefs enter lions, and lions, as well as the smaller cats, are thought to be employed as messengers by witches, much as the cat is associated with witchcraft in European lore. But the lion was not invincible. A Zambian folk story (which seems to have crossed the Atlantic with African slaves and found its way into the stories of Uncle Remus) tells how the Hare outwitted the King of Beasts.

The Lion was afraid of fire but one day when he was out walking with the Hare, the Hare told him that he had a magic potion that made him invulnerable to fire. 'Show me,' said the Lion, so the smaller animal lay down on an ant-hill and asked the Lion to set fire to the surrounding grass which was tinder-dry. As soon as the flames obscured him from the Lion's sight he slipped down a burrow underground, then, as the flames died down, he came out and rolled in the ash to look as though he had been in the fire. When he saw that the Hare

Above Amur leopard, now surviving only in North Korea and the Lake Khamka area north of Vladivostock. **Left** A black panther, actually a melanistic form of the leopard and not a separate species. **Opposite page** Lion and lioness

had not come to any harm the Lion demanded that he share the secret. 'Very well,' said the Hare, 'Look, here is another ant-hill covered in dry grass. You must lie down in the middle and I will light the fire.' 'But, first you must tell me the secret,' said the Lion. 'Of course, here are some magic leaves. You must eat these, and remember to stand quite still even though the flames feel as though they singe your fur.'

The Hare set fire to the grass and the flames got hotter and hotter round the Lion so that he roared loudly in alarm but the Hare told him to be quiet or it would spoil the magic power of the leaves. So the Lion stood still as the fire burned his fur and blistered his skin and the heat and smoke suffocated him, and the Lion died.

When the flames died down and he was sure the Lion was dead, the Hare ran off to tell the other beasts that he had killed the Lion and now he was king.

There are many variations of the following South American Indian story.

Lions and lionesses have very individual characters and can be as playful and affectionate as any domestic cat

A boy was trapped high up on a cliff while trying to steal birds' eggs. When he was nearly dead from thirst and hunger a jaguar passed by beneath and saw him. The jaguar leaned a tree against the cliff and rescued the boy. He took him on his back and carried him to a creek where the boy drank as much as he wanted and fell asleep. At last the jaguar woke him up and washed him and told him that as he had no children of his own he would adopt the boy as his own son.

When they got to the jaguar's house there was a big log burning on the floor. 'What is that?' asked the boy. 'That is fire,' answered the jaguar 'at night it will keep you warm my son, and it will cook your food,' and he gave the boy a piece of roast meat that his wife had cooked. And so the boy slept in the jaguar's house.

Next morning the jaguar went hunting. When the boy felt hungry he asked the jaguar's wife for food, but she refused him and bared her teeth. When the boy told him the jaguar rebuked his wife, then he produced a bow and arrow which he taught the boy to use. Another night passed and again the jaguar went hunting but when his wife threatened him, the boy took the bow and arrow and shot her dead.

When the jaguar returned he was not angry that his wife was dead but gave the boy roast meat and told him how to return to his village. When the boy reached home he told everyone of his adventures and the village decided to set out to find the fire. The jaguar gladly gave it to them for, as he told the boy's true father, 'I have adopted your son.'

Other versions tell how the Indians returned and stole the fire and that the jaguar, angered by the ingratitude of his adopted son to whom he had given the secrets of fire and of the bow and arrow, renounced them both so that now he is full of hatred for humanity, hunts with his fangs and eats his meat raw.

Among the Navaho Indians of New Mexico and Arizona the bear, the puma and the wildcat are linked as benefactors of man, for one of their legends tells how the great creator mother Estanatlehui, their most respected deity, sent these animals to hunt for the Navaho and protect them.

Christian legend tends to reverse the roles and shows man helping the animals. The most famous story is probably that of Androcles, a Roman slave who found a lion howling with pain and extracted a large thorn from its paw. Later, having been converted to Christianity, he was thrown to the beasts in a Roman amphitheater. To the spectators' amazement the lion which was expected to tear him limb from limb stopped in its tracks, recognized his benefactor and purring began to lick his face, so impressing the emperor that Androcles' life was spared and the lion freed.

The jaguar is the largest of the South American cats. The baby, **above**, was photographed at only four months old and was the first to be born at London Zoo

The same act of kindness is the beginning of the almost identical stories told about St. Gerasimus and of St. Jerome, both of whom were abbots of monasteries by the River Jordan. Perhaps the legend about St. Gerasimus was later accredited to the better-known saint who gave the world the Latin Vulgate bible.

One day the holy abbot Gerasimus was walking by the Jordan when he came upon a mighty lion throwing back its head and roaring loudly as if in pain. As the saint approached the beast limped towards him on three legs and stood before him whimpering and holding out a paw which was swollen and festering. The abbot had compassion on the lion and sat beside him without fear. Taking the injured foot in his hands he saw that embedded in it was a sharp piece of reed. Speaking gently to the lion he cut the swollen flesh with a knife, removed the reed and squeezed the poisonous matter from the wound. Then with a piece of cloth he cleaned and bound the wound and sent the lion away.

But the grateful lion would not leave the holy man and followed him back to the monastery, where the monks first fled in terror, then stood amazed at the gentleness and gratitude of the beast. Thereafter the lion lived in the monastery and was fed by Gerasimus and the monks on bread and herbs. Everyone must make their contribution to a monastic community and the lion was given the task of keeping guard over the donkey which drew water. One hot day, after the donkey had drawn the day's water from the well, the lion was watching it grazing, when he fell asleep. At just that time a camel driver came by and saw the donkey. He could not see the lion and, seizing the donkey's halter, dragged it away to lead

It is not only in legends that lions have made close friends of human beings. Lions raised in captivity can become very attached to people

the camels of his caravan, as was the custom in those times. When the lion awoke the donkey was nowhere to be seen. He searched and searched and then returned dejected to the monastery.

'Where is the donkey?' abbot Gerasimus asked. But all that the lion could do was lower his head and the abbot assumed that he had returned to his natural ways. 'So, you have eaten the ass. In recompense whatever the ass did, that must you do.'

The lion could not explain that he had not eaten the donkey, but he had failed in his duty so he allowed himself to be put into the ass's harness and for four years drew the water from the well. Then a soldier came to the abbot for blessing and seeing the king of beasts at his menial task gave money to the monastery to purchase a new ass. Not long after, the camel driver passed by the monastery again. He saw the new donkey in the field and thought to steal this one as well, but as he approached the lion sprang out at him and he ran as fast as his legs could carry him. The man ran back to his camels but still the lion came after him so he ran on and plunged into the Jordan. Then the lion recognized the ass leading the camels as his former charge, and taking his halter between his teeth led donkey and camels to the monastery. Roaring jubilantly, he sought out the old abbot to show him what he had done, and the abbot saw that he had wronged the lion and named the lion Jordanus.

For five more years Jordanus lived among the monks following in the old man's footsteps when he was not with the donkeys. At last came the time for Gerasimus to be called to his maker. When the abbot was lowered to his rest the lion was nowhere to be seen. On his return Jordanus searched everywhere for his old master and when the new abbot told him that Gerasimus was with the Lord, and bade him eat, the lion would not. Jordanus would not accept the new abbot's comfort, the more he ruffled his mane and offered consolation, the more piteously the lion roared. So the abbot took Jordanus and showed him where his master was buried. When he knelt beside the spot the lion lay down and beat his head upon the ground and there Jordanus died, upon holy Gerasimus' grave.

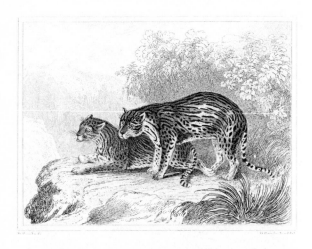

Top Ocelot. **Above** Lynx. **Top right** Leopard
Right Tiger. **Opposite page, top** Lion
Bottom left Jaguar. **Bottom right** Cheetah

Before photography, illustrations of big cats varied from the fanciful to meticulously detailed anatomical drawings, but species were often confused and animals in the wild incorrectly identified. There is still a great deal to be learned about the lives of members of the cat family

The cheetah is the fastest of land animals and always gives the appearance of being alert. Its lithe figure and characteristic mask make identification easy

The youngest of these cats and cubs are the two seen with their mother, **top**, and are scarcely two and a half months old

How the hare outwitted the king of beasts

A story from the Hausa of Nigeria

One day all the animals on whom the lion used to prey got together to see how they could defend themselves. 'He is bigger and stronger than any of us,' they said, 'how can we save ourselves?' Perhaps if the lion were allowed to eat one of them each day without having to hunt he might leave the rest alone. The lion is a lazy animal and he agreed, so the animals drew lots to see who should be the first.

The fatal lot was drawn by the gazelle and next day she was taken by the animals to where the lion was and left, terrified, to be his meal. The lion killed and ate her and that day he did not harm the other animals. Each day another animal had to offer itself as a victim for the lion until at last the turn of the hare arrived.

Animals on which lions prey, such as the wildebeest caught by the lioness, **right**, seem to know whether lions are hungry or not, and often graze close to a party of lions without showing any apparent concern. However at the first sign of aggressive interest, they will take evasive action

The hare stood as tall and proud as he could manage and told the other animals that he was not frightened and they would not have to take him to the lion—he would go there on his own—and off he went. But he did not go to the lion, he went back home and took a nap. When none of the animals arrived the lion began to get hungry and set out to look for his dinner. His roaring woke the hare who climbed into a tree overlooking a well. When the lion passed by, the hare called out and asked him why he was making so much noise. The lion complained that his promised meal had not arrived, so the hare told him that he was the chosen meal and that as a special treat he had been taking a pot of honey with him as a present, when he had been frightened by another lion who had taken the honey.

'When I told him it was for you,' the hare went on, 'he said he didn't care, he is not afraid of you because he is much stronger than you.'

'Where is this other lion?'

'He is taking a rest in the cool of that well,' the hare replied.

At that the lion looked down the well and saw there was indeed another lion. He roared at him in challenge and waited for his reply—but the other lion said nothing. The lion roared again and got very angry. When the other lion still just stared back at him he jumped into the well to attack the insolent animal—and was drowned. Then the hare climbed down from the tree and went back to the other animals.

'I have killed the lion,' he told them. 'Now I am the King of Beasts.'

Both lions and tigers occasionally turn man-eater.
Human beings have never been their natural prey,
but if they should kill a man or woman in
defending themselves or their young they may
eat, and acquire a taste for human flesh, or, more

likely, will discover how comparatively easy
it is to kill or overcome this animal on two legs.
Illness and old age, which make it difficult
to hunt, play their part in turning them to preying
on man